A Yankee Crosses The Wide Río Grande
By Thomas R. Gagnon

Published by Thomas R. Gagnon, 1995. All rights reserved. Printed in the United States of America. No part of this book may be used or reproduced in any manner whatsoever without written permission except in the case of brief quotations embodied in critical articles and reviews. For information write P.O. Box 6, Bond, Colorado 80423.

First Printing 1995 (4)
Second Printing 1995 (100)
Third Printing 1996 (500)
Fourth Printing 1996 (1000)

ISBN 0-9652571-2-6

Copyright 08051371 (1996)

Cover Art by Troy Tuggle

To Joseph, wish you were here on the Colorado River.
Tom Gagnon
8-98

Table of Contents

Preface .... *v.*
Acknowledgments .... *vi.*

Trip One: December 18, 1991, to January 10, 1992

Chapter I.	Traveling South	2
Chapter II.	The Heart of Oaxaca	16
Chapter III.	On the Coast	25
Chapter IV.	A Journey Through History	46

Trip Two: January 15, 1993, to April 25, 1993

Chapter V.	Returning South	62
Chapter VI.	Welcome to Guatemala.	81
Chapter VII.	Adrift in Central America	101
Chapter VIII.	Nicaragua	119
Chapter IX.	Two Wars, Economy, and Timing	127
Chapter X.	Honduras	132
Chapter XI.	Antigua Life	141
Chapter XII.	To the Continental Divide in the Department of San Marcos	157
Chapter XIII.	The Capital and Mataquescuintla	177
Chapter XIV.	The Cuchumatán Highlands	182

Epilogue

Chapter XV.	The Machete	194

To: My Little Brothers
in
La Unión, El Salvador

Preface

This book is a travelogue. Besides the scenic beauty and urban sights that I have described, and the many adventures that I recount -some humorous, some enlightening, some deadly, and always surprising- I have packed it with historical and cultural information.

Travelers are only the most obvious that might benefit from this book. They can use it as a general guide. Those that find México and Central America a giant, inexplicable mystery, as I once did, will be pleased to discover that it is comprehensible after all.

Most of the measurements and amounts are approximations. México and the Central American countries use the metric system, and for that reason I have used it south of the Río Grande too, while often providing conversions for the convenience of people from the United States.

Most of the names of people are actual. However, in a few cases, where I thought that a name change might be appreciated, I have done so.

Acknowledgments

This book would not have been possible without the many people that have kindly helped me along in so many ways. Of the people in Colorado that helped and encouraged me: The staff of the Avon Public Library is extraordinarily helpful, I thank them and the town for providing the computer on which much of this book was written; my friends at Rancho del Río have been patient with a writer's rent, and insightful; Dr. Michael Fry of Fort Lewis College, Durango, has taught me much and has given me many ideas for this book, concerning security, I wish that I had followed his advice always, and, he has been a friend; in an indirect way, but important to the development of my way of looking at other cultures and political systems, is Dr. Thomas R. Eckenrode, also of Fort Lewis College; Ken Wright and his wife Sarah have often provided a roof over my head, and, over cigars, beer, and around an old miner's uranium bucket containing a campfire, on a U.F.O. landing strip, Ken has taught me much about writing; Marsha Peters, Lance George, Rick Gogan and Jeff Smith have been invaluable proofreaders; Art Krizman and Mark Aaron Peters provided technical support; Patti Fisher provided much needed encouragement; and I owe much to many other Coloradans as well.

Along the way in New Mexico and Texas, and throughout México, Guatemala, El Salvador, Nicaragua, and Honduras, there are many people that I am beyond the ability to thank either directly or sufficiently, their lives, manners, good dispositions, and humor, have been lessons in life for me.

In Chapter XV, though a grim ending in many ways, I thank all the people mentioned therein, especially Terri and

Cristi Vielman, who took care of me; Lieneke Poelman for companionship and encouragement during trying days; and Dr. José del Valle Monge, who read and corrected the Spanish in the manuscript of this book, and who came to me in my time of need; and to his brother, Dr. Carlos del Valle Monge, who saved my hands.

I would like to thank Steve Pappenheim of Boston, for his encouragement and ideas. In New Hampshire, I would like to thank Dr. John Sherwin, and hand therapists Kathleen Hanlon and Diane DeLorme for their follow-up care in restoring my hands. Thanks also go to Joelle Pinard, Jimmy Lehoux, and Denis Gagnon, for help with something that I will never understand, computers; many other family members have also been extremely helpful, including my brother Ron, who mobilized his entire accounting firm (during Tax Season) to the task of completing this book; and, finally, I thank my parents, Ronald and Constance, my brothers and their families, for rescuing and taking care of me in the lowest days of my life. I apologize for anyone that I have overlooked. Any mistakes or misunderstandings in this book are solely of my own doing.

TRIP ONE

December, 18, 1991
to
January, 10, 1992

I.
Traveling South

To professor and classmates I announced, *"Ahora voy a México"* (Now I go to México) as I left the room at the end of the final. It was December 18, 1991, at Fort Lewis College in Durango, Colorado. It was my first "successfully" completed semester of Spanish. Soon I was on the road. It took two rides to get to Farmington, New Mexico. From there a student, recently returned from Spain, gave me a ride to Albuquerque. I doubt the wheels ever touched the ground and we arrived in New Mexico's largest city at 3:30 P.M. He dropped me off at the Albuquerque International Hostel.

It was my last day of my 20s, and I was still "hosteling," as they say in the Old World. As if to celebrate the impending day of doom, the hostel desk clerk was passionately strumming on a guitar while a German was playing the piano. Their jazz was outstanding. Other hostlers seemed to agree and gathered around. The crowd of a dozen represented five countries. The atmosphere was worth the hundreds of miles I had traveled. I had started traveling while in Europe at age nineteen. Not much had changed since then, only now I was traveling on my own continent. As terrific as Europe is, I suspect that it receives too much attention from the United States. In the United States, after all, on the psychological map of the world, the Río Grande is wider than the North Atlantic.

Next day it took only four rides to get to the border. In fact, I was dropped off by two Texans right at the crossing. One of them reminded me to say my prayers "down there." I replied that I would pray more than usual for the next three weeks. Though it was a strange thing for an agnostic to say, I was SCARED. So many people had told me horror stories about Mexican "law." That was it I thought, "I might as well turn myself in for being innocent; save some Mexican cop the trouble of planting dope on me."

The bridge was of the high arc persuasion. From there one could see the two cities at the base of sheer ranges of rocky mountains. I thought the engineers built it that way to give me a good look at the two options. One was modern and rich, the other, from what I could see of Ciudad Juarez, was absolutely impoverished. The only dilapidated thing on the U.S. side was a rusted, partly cut through and in places ripped down double row of chain link fence. Below trickled the Río Grande (or, the Río Bravo.) It was not an ordinary day here at the border. The bridge's sidewalks were packed, and the bumpers in the four lanes of traffic were nearly grinding each other. With one final look at my own country, still not too late to go back, I turned and plunged forth.

There was no elaborate customs station, nor anyone in uniform. The Mexicans were completely indifferent to my entry. A week before leaving Colorado I had looked at a map of Juarez, so I knew that the train station was exactly ten blocks straight down the road -that is, if I had crossed the right bridge. Wandering around for about thirty blocks, I finally gave up my minimal-Spanish-induced shyness and started asking people directions. In that way I got to see a fair bit of Juarez.

Many and varied small businesses lined the streets. Those nearest the border were dental offices. Dozens of small sidewalk stands spilt over the curbs and added to the congestion. Many of the shops in the first five or so blocks were geared toward tourists that happened to be in El Paso, and the curiosity of another country got them to cross over for an hour. There were leather shops, and an endless variety of souvenirs were available. The Mexicans carried all assortments of packages, many in distinctive U.S. department store over-packaging, plus boxes tied in twine, burlap bags, old Samsonites, even buckets. It was the beginning of the holidays and everyone was scurrying to purchase gifts and travel home. Juarez is home to few, but an encampment for about a million people that mostly come from north-central México. With the possibility of earning a wage in a U.S. company's *maquiladora* (a factory), Juarez represents an opportunity for them. However, I thought, and I met Mexicans that agreed with me, it's a dubious prospect.[1] Apparently, I had arrived just in time to pack the trains with them and go south.

Finally at the station, with my propensity for short cuts, I chose the shortest line. Within ten minutes I was at a window where a man directed me to another line. Working at the desk was a woman who spoke some English. There I learnt that all the trains were filled until six the next morning, and that I had to go back into town to exchange travelers checks at a *casa de cambio* (house of exchange). My understanding of this information did not come easily, though it emerged into a comic situation. It involved the efforts of many people helping to stitch together a few lines of English, while I tried to speedily page through a Spanish/English dictionary amidst a swaying sea of people. There were also the hand directional signs and facial expressions -

---

[1] *U.S. labor and environmental laws do not apply in these places, and Mexican laws are less restrictive. This leads to working conditions and pollution not commonly seen in the U.S. for several decades.*

probably more effective than words- thus a chaotic communication was established.

As a train pulled away, a calm descended upon the station. I met the people around me. In fact, I was such an oddity to the Mexicans that many of them wanted to know me. They found it very unusual for a U.S. citizen to be traveling alone by train, and prepared to sleep in the station with them. Most foreigners on vacation in México travel by air, car, or at the very least, by first class bus. I spoke at length with a lady who had been particularly helpful with translation. She was beshawled and had a kind grandmotherly look. She was very well read and her main interests were in sociology, economics and politics. I also made the acquaintance of Francisco and Vincent. Francisco was a mechanic from Torréon. Vincent worked illegally in Texas as a ranch laborer. He was heading home to Parral for the holidays. Vincent and I went into town.

In the city that night, I doubt I could have found my way to the *cambio* without Vincent's help. We stopped for dinner at a sidewalk stand that had a few feet of overhang that kept us dry when the rain started. It poured. Soon the streets were curb deep in water. Lightning pounded overhead. Three men worked behind the counter, Vincent was laughing heartily with them. As many people crowded under the canopy a carnival atmosphere ensued. In a good mood and energized by a nearby bolt of lightning, I couldn't resist yelling out "*¡Pancho Villa esta en las montañas!*" (It's Pancho Villa in the mountains!). The people around roared with laughter and Vincent slapped me on the back.

When the rain stopped we started back for the station. Most of the streets, however, were flooded. Like log jams, cars were not moving, but their fenders made ledges to cross the deepest waters. Some folks in a station wagon from north of the border hollered at Vincent and I when we made use of their bumper. Mexicans just smiled and waved when we walked on their bumpers. One man tied plastic shopping bags over his shoes. He crossed a road and seemed to emerge dry. It wasn't long before Vincent and I did the same. We stayed dry for quite a while. Unfortunately, though, in a steep street that had more water running down it than some rivers that I've rafted on, the bags finally came off. Right before getting to the station there was an unavoidable thigh deep street pond. Vincent was self conscious and apologetic about the flood, as he felt that it was what should have been expected of a "lesser" country than mine, I told him that I hadn't felt so alive in a long time, and that with the amount of rain we got, this would happen anywhere.

In the early morning I bought a ticket for Ciudad de México (Mexico City). The train departed in the predawn. The cost was merely 49,200 pesos,[2] for a distance of some 2,000 kilometers (1,240 miles.) A red, orange, and yellow sunrise over the Mexican Plateau, with the jagged peaks of the Sierra Madre Oriental on the horizon, greeted the new day. By then, however, I was becoming an unwilling center of attraction. I had been up talking to people most of the night. Now I just wanted to sleep. The seats were the type found on school buses. It was amazing that people could sleep on them at all, but everyone did.

Upon awakening, my seat mate bought me a Tecate. He had worked in the U.S. off and on for the last twelve years, including an apple picking stint in Paonia, Colorado.

---

[2]*$1.00 U.S. was roughly equivalent to 3,000. pesos.*

He told me that the Mexicans on the train were happy to see me, as second class on the train usually didn't carry "whites or rich people," and that I treated them as equals, and in a friendly way. His English was pretty good; he told me that the English he knew was referred to as "*jefe inglés*" (the boss' English), or, that which one learns from a foreman yelling at you all day.

Sixteen year old Sandra was going home to a farm town in Coahuila for the holidays. In Juarez she had an assembly plant job. Two years earlier she had to quit school to support herself and send money to her mother. I asked her if she was happy with her job, if she planned to ever go back to school, and what her plans were for the future. To these questions she answered that she knew many good jobs were being lost in the United States, and bad jobs were being created in México. For that reason she felt both guilty and taken advantage of. She said that although she could earn more working in a *maquiladora,* it was expensive to live near the border, and that she was lonely since her family lived so far away. To the next question she simply said that getting back to school was a "difficult situation," although I had no doubts about her intellect. To my final inquiry, she answered that she was curious about the United States, and would like to see it, but that she was afraid of crime there.

In other conversations, the Mexicans were interested in where I was from, as well as the college I attended, and my interest in Latin American history. To the latter question, I answered that it was strictly an accident, one college course to fill a "requirement," and I was amazed to discover that a region with a superlative history, people, and landscape existed adjacent to my own country. My earlier education had hardly mentioned Latin America. They were also interested in my summer rafting job and how dangerous it was. To this I had to confess that where I raft, the rapids are really not too tough. Most of all, though, they wanted to know about my family, and why I had not taken my girlfriend with me.

As packed as the train had been in the evening, at night we stopped to pick up even more people. I couldn't write then as the car did not have lighting. Luckily, many people detrained before daylight. On the bumpy and rocky ride I saw many acts of kindness and trust. People switched off in seats to give each other breaks from standing in the aisle. One feeble and poor looking elderly man traveling alone had lost his ticket, I knew he had had one since I saw it earlier when he showed it to a conductor. When a different conductor demanded to see it, he couldn't find it and nervously started looking for it under his seat. A man in work clothes intervened and bought the old timer a new ticket. When the train became so crowded that no one could move, women who were lucky enough to be seated held the babies of women that had to stand.

"México's greatest strength is its people," is a common saying. From what I saw it's true. However, from what I came to understand, some of México's biggest problems are its long ruling P.R.I. (Institutional Revolutionary Party) politicians, and its dependent economic position with the United States. Bearing this in mind, my hope was that the accommodating and patient Mexicans did not extend their cooperative qualities to the government, and the situation that was keeping them from obtaining equitable political rights, such as fair elections and an adequate material lifestyle. However, I did see some signs of conflict.

A rock cracked one of the state owned train windows

as we entered a Chihuahuan town. All the decrepit houses, constructed of fifty-five gallon drums, odd sized timbers, rocks, cinder blocks, tar paper, and corrugated tin, had one bright spot: On the smoothest surface of each house, in full view of the train, were yellow "P.T." (Workers' Party) letters, with a yellow star above, on a red background. This represented a radical labor position, and probably for good reason, but I never again saw anything like it in México. It didn't look like the local communists were triumphing, further along we passed a huge ultra modern factory, it was enclosed in a concentration camp like fence topped with barbed wire, and had spot lights on tall poles all around. Through other towns in the north, other signs of discontent in graffiti were manifest in crossed out "P.R.I." signs on buildings and walls, versus well kept "P.A.N." signs (National Action Party).

    The next morning I awoke to cool, fresh air, and the sight of giant twelve foot tall nopal cacti (resembling giant prickly pear cacti), Joshua trees, maguey plants (giant yucca or aloe looking plants), and many shrubs and low growing trees. Coming to the top of a climb from a wild valley, the train emerged onto a flat upland. There were many small farms, which contrasted with the large dry-land ranches up north.

    Our train stopped at a siding near a *campesino* village. One man was rhythmically chopping away at some stumps in front of a house. Some children were helping each other carry large buckets of corn seed. A portly woman, in a bright-red shawl, was walking around chatting a little with each neighbor as though on inspection or gathering news.

    Perhaps owing to the vegetation, the area seemed less littered than the far northern country. In México, trash is simply tossed anywhere. When there were few people on board, the conductor swept all the garbage from under the seats, then down the long aisle to the opened doors at the ends of the car. Even that town received our dumpings. Until recently, most garbage in México was biodegradable. For instance, most food was wrapped in banana and other large leaves, now it's packed in plastic and aluminum foil. Therefore, previously, "littering" only enriched the soil, now it poisons it. Culture is always a few steps behind its own technology.

The train went downhill gently and the farms grew larger. The freshly tilled soil was rich looking. Large machinery worked the land. The train pulled into Aguascalientes (Hot Waters, i.e., hot springs,) the capital of the state of that name. It was the nicest place in México I had seen up to that point. We stopped at the train station for about twenty minutes. I got off the train to look around. The station was clean and was not overly crowded. Several vendors were selling food and drinks. They walked through the train or stood outside to hand their products through windows, they sold to people walking around the station stretching their legs.

My one quart water container had gone dry some time ago. I was thirsty. Many of the Mexicans were buying water from a lady with five gallon plastic buckets. They had "MOBIL" written on them. The water in one bucket was lime green, in the other it was strawberry red. Both had particles of the fruits used to sweeten and taint them. The water was simply ladled out and poured into plastic bags of about half a liter, and a straw was added. I bought one of each. First I tried the green water. I wanted to suck it down and quench my thirst, but I could only drink half as it tasted really bad. The strawberry tasted better and refreshed me. At that time I did not know that mineral and distilled water in bottles was available.

    The train pulled into Ciudad de México at midnight of the twenty second. In an exhausted and poor state of mind, I went to what was either the Central Hotel or Garage Hotel. The neon signs outside didn't make clear exactly what the name was. I thought of the dry inn keeper as "Mr. Personality." He hated me. A few days before I waited some fourteen hours to board a train, then the ride was a staggering forty-two hours long. I was tired and my stomach was upset.

    I slept many needed hours, until 1:00 P.M. I felt rested, but my stomach was worse than the day before. Hotel check out was at 2:00. As it was Sunday, changing currency would be difficult, yet my need was immediate. I wanted one more night there, I knew I couldn't face another train right away. So, I set out looking for the only *cambio* that was open that day. That such a place was open at all, I only knew from the laborers on the street. They pooled their English and picked through my Spanish. Then they directed me to a bus stop.

    The first driver was very kind and the five hundred peso ride was *gratis*. The next bus took me to near where I needed to be, but I mistook the driver's directions. About to hop on another bus for a ride to who knows where, looking around like the lost child I was, I saw looming nearby the word "Liverpool," and near that "Parisur." The first word, being English, captured my eye. The second sounded a lot like the place the workers were trying to send me to. Suddenly everything clicked. Apparently, Parisur is a large and chic shopping mall. It was encircled by expensive cars, and all about the place were elegantly dressed people. Liverpool is a department store carrying British fashions and products.

The pace in Parisur was much faster than anyplace I had seen in México. Being near Christmas it was very busy. Everyone but me was well dressed at the *cambio*. People had handfuls of U.S. dollars in big denominations. The guards looked me over with suspicion as I exchanged a fifty dollar traveler's check. I went back to the bus stop and dined curb side with my economic kindred.

There was a beautiful park where I had to change buses. I took a walk in it. By then I was so late on payment for my room that I figured Mr. Personality could wait another half hour. Catching a bus would be no problem as they came along Avenida Insurgentes approximately every minute. In the park stands a monument to President (1920-24) and Mexican Revolutionary General Alvaro Obregon. He was the consolidator of that bloody episode, a sort of Mexican Napoleon. As Obregon had lost an arm to a cannonball during the pivotal Battle of Celaya, in 1915, the theme of the monument is "sacrifice for the nation," and his massive arm is preserved behind a glass for all to see.

At 4:30 I arrived back at my room and discovered all my belongings... still there. Mr. Personality hadn't thrown my things out on the street. By then, though, my stomach was turning some olympian somersaults. Time for a break. About 7:00 I was feeling weak and dehydrated. Surprisingly, although I didn't mind the city, I was determined to leave it as soon as possible since I felt its air pollution was making me sick. Plus, the hotel room was depressing and windowless. I planned to leave for Oaxaca at 7:00 the next evening by first class train.

Though most of the people I met were friendly, I felt out of my element in the world's largest city. I had a U.S. Shakey's Restaurant to thank for rescuing my stomach and attitude that night. It had a clean bathroom with a seat! It was the first such that I had seen in México. Between their mineral water and facilities I was feeling much better. For the next day I planed to visit the Universidad Nacional Autónoma[3] de México (National Autonomous University of México, commonly known as Ciudad Universitavia or University City) before leaving.

I was sick that night, however. Very sick! At least I lost a few pounds. I checked out of my hotel room as planned and bought the train ticket, but other plans for the day fell through as I felt too weak to do anything other than loiter at Shakey's and the train station. Slowing down, just looking and listening, was probably good, though, so that my thoughts could catch up to all the things that were new to me.

In the station I put my finger on something that had been staring me right in the face, yet it had been too obvious to notice: CHILDREN, pregnant women, and women of child bearing age. They were everywhere, beautiful, and always audible. Baby making seems to be the national sport. I wondered what these babies would do for work one day. Although more manufacturing jobs are coming to México from the U.S., albeit mostly low in pay, I doubt that jobs created will keep pace with the exploding population. A rapidly expanding population seems to have been partly

---

[3]*The word* Autónoma *(Autonomous) is found in the names of many Latin American Universities, and its interpretation is a touchy issue. It implies that the school is its own corporate and sovereign entity, thus, any opinions can be voiced, for or against the government, and government troops are not allowed on the premises.*

responsible for neutralizing and reversing some of the reforms of the Mexican Revolution of 1910 to 1920. The school system, for example, could not be expanded quickly enough to provide education for those that had never had it before, such as most of the country's Indians, and keep pace with population growth.

I had chosen first class due to my physical condition. This train was very different from the Juarez train. It had lighting, airline type chairs, spaciousness, some suspension, no one stood in the aisles, food and drinks were served, and many of the kids in this class of travel had Walkmans and other gadgets. It was much more comfortable than second class had been, and I got the sleep I needed. Also, my attitude improved.

The vast differences in trains demonstrates the several economic classes of Mexicans. Since crossing the border, I had seen people that probably didn't take any trains. They were the ones in abject poverty: The winos of the Juarez train yard; many of the *campesinos* in the fields off to the side of the tracks; and the sick panhandling lady with the filthy child squatting on a sidewalk.

Then there were the industrial working class, and those that steal across the U.S. border to earn $10.00 to $20.00 a day working on farms and ranches. These people ride the trains in second class, living hard, tough lives. Their marginal level of living is totally dependent upon their physical condition. These are the people that I associated with most. They seem to look up to the educated, especially university students, and teachers; yet most of them, I inferred, were unable to stay in school beyond about age fourteen as the immediate problem of earning a living called loudly.[4] I didn't speak to any of these people about religion, but outward signs on their persons, such as rosaries and crucifixes, attest to their beliefs and faith.

Then there were the chic, like the people sitting before and after me in first class, though perhaps they were only bourgeoisie; the really rich travel by air. James A. Michener, in Iberia, put it succinctly by saying that only India outdoes the Spanish world in the area of social class stratification.

---

[4]*In México, less than 5 percent of intellectuals come from working-class backgrounds. By contrast, in the U.S., 40 percent come from this class. Charles Kadushin's American Intellectual Elite, (Boston: Little, Brown, 1974), 26, in Roderic Ai Camp's Politics in México, (Oxford U.P., 1993) 23.*

II.
The Heart of Oaxaca

I awoke on the train to the sight of cliffs descending to a tumbling stream in a canyon. There were *milpas* -small corn plots rotated back into use every so many years depending on soil conditions. These were on river gravel flats and steep hillsides. The soil was not very fertile looking, and it had a lot of rocks. Emerging onto the Oaxaca Plateau, the soil looked thick and dark. Farms with goats, donkeys, horses and diminutive cattle were plentiful. A combination of trucks, animal drawn carts, and plows were used. Small irrigation ditches and aqueducts crisscrossed the land. Farmers stopped working to wave at the train. The P.R.I. advertisements were well kept; here the Revolution had not gone too bitter. There was a more contented atmosphere in this part of México. It is a proud place, too, for this is the birthplace of Benito Juarez, pure blooded Zapotec and incorruptible president of México, and leader of its resistance to the French occupation in the 1860s.

On the train I met Tim and Jujuy. The first was about fifteen and living in Guadalajara for two years . His dad was with a church doing missionary work. In the States they live in Bend, Oregon. Jujuy is Mexican, eighteen, and works in Guadalajara.

Oaxaca's train station is old, very clean, and beautiful. Large trees surround it and the air was warm and dry. The town hadn't changed much since the colonial era. The markets in town were bustling, perhaps something to do with the approach of Christmas. For Christmas, I planned to be in town to see a real Mexican celebration.

From the train station, Tim, Jujuy, and I went straight to the hotel where you can get a bus to the ruins of Monte Albán. This is an historic site, abandoned and returned to nature long before the Spanish conquest. It was refreshing to meet "Mexican tourists" for a change. I met four people from the state of Oaxaca, and one from Ciudad de México, who were doing just as I was.

On the bus I met George, a Japanese/Britisher. We explored the ruins together. From the mountain that the ruins are perched, four hundred meters (1,300 feet) above the surface of the Oaxaca Plateau, the view is of agricultural lands all around, and large but not steep mountains encircling. The passages within the ruins are deep and dark, I regretted that I had not taken a flashlight, as almost every passage was open to the public for exploring.

Monte Albán was designed by skilled architects, and built with the toil of many. The site is a kilometer long. Most of the ruins are elongated pyramids of shoulder high tiers, which are connected by steps ascending to flat tops. These were once crowned by wooden buildings. On rock surfaces there are perplexing bas-relief *Danzantes* (Dancers), men that look like specimens in a formaldehyde limbo. Set between high walls is a typical Mesoamerican **I** shaped ball court, where a game somewhat resembling basketball was played, only losing seems to have meant death. Of the most significant intellectual interest, there is evidence of the "Calendar Round's" employment, which, when used together with the "Long Count," makes for an accurate way of recording time.

One of the mysteries of the ruins, so high above any source of water, is, how did they get water to the numerous workers that built it? Another question is that although other sites in the area were built about the same time, why are their artistic creations so completely different? Were they rivals? One theory holds that at Monte Albán's height, sixty thousand people inhabited the site. I had no trouble believing that the bulk of the population lived down on the plain, but the mountaintop must have only been for officials and ceremonies.

In the current day, the up-side of the tourist industry is that many people can now see the hard evidence that many pre-Columbian Americans were as capable of living in metropolitan civilizations as Europeans, and not all were hunters and gatherers. In this sense, the reconstructed stone work here is very positive, otherwise, nature would obliterate an historic site as important to humans for understanding themselves as the Egyptian pyramids or the Great Wall of China. Although the ruins of America mostly hold mysteries, their stones tell no lies.

On the down-side of the tourist industry there are Zapotecs from the locale selling art artifacts within the site. Aside from being annoying, the Zapotecs had dug up these figurines at nearby archeological sites (although many may be forgeries.) They were selling their history. It would have been like myself finding an artifact of Charlemagne and taking money for it, instead of giving it to a museum in Aix-la-Chapelle. The large number of tourists seemed to be sapping the place of its exotic atmosphere.

On a ridge below Monte Albán, Jujuy, Tim, and I camped with a view of Ciudad Oaxaca below. Where walkers on the trail wore the grass down, the ground was covered and composed of a thick layer of pottery shards. Although some pieces were large and had beautiful designs, they now served as gravel. When it got dark and the city lights came on, fire crackers exploded every few seconds.

After my best night's sleep since Colorado, my two companions and I walked down from our camping perch. In the center of town, as planned, we met George at a bar. Tim and Jujuy set off to continue their journey to Chiapas and the ruins of Palenque. Caught with exchanges closed, George lent me fifty thousand pesos. He was a good companion in town. He had traveled a lot and was well educated, yet out of place almost everywhere, and not just a little restless to "get on with life." One thing confusing him was what to do with a twenty-eight year old girlfriend back in Japan. Being single beyond age twenty-two in that country was considered odd. She wanted to marry, and planed to join him hereabouts in March.

The central area of some Mexican cities have what's called a *zócalo*. Oaxaca's is about three blocks in size and includes a park with giant trees and shrubbery, a bandstand, and cobbled walkways and patios. As it is in the state of Oaxaca's largest city and capital, around it are various government buildings, banks, churches, a cathedral, as well as the area's finer restaurants. Of the latter, there's sidewalk seating in addition to the elegant indoor dinning. In the park there was a Nativity with three quarter sized donkeys, cows, sheep, shepherds, wise men, Joseph, the Virgin Mary, and the baby Jesus in a stray crib under a roof of boards and hay. Parents were out with their children and all looked on the scene with reverence and affection.

Our hotel was several blocks from the *zócalo,* and accordingly inexpensive. George's room cost thirty thousand pesos per night, and mine, although identical, was for some inexplicable reason only ten thousand. I didn't complain. George and I wandered the city streets and made many discoveries off the tourist frequented strips. We entered a *mercado* (market.) There we walked down a long smoky hallway with every variety of red meat, chicken, and pork. Some meat was being smoked for storage, but most was grilled for selling and eating on the spot. At the other end of the hall a tall and open warehouse thronged with people shopping and sitting at the counters of dozens of small cafés. Each café also specialized in a product such as cheese, bread, fruit, vegetables, candy and nuts. The people were unhurriedly socializing. Eating there was inexpensive and we ate to our hearts' content. I only met one person that spoke English, and he told me that the restaurants on the *zócalo* bought their food at the *mercado*.

Making stops at bars in the *zócalo* that evening, George and I spoke to other foreigners. Some had first-class bus tickets for the coast, for which they paid about sixty thousand pesos. They were complaining that México was more expensive than they had planned on, and the "safe" food in the *zócalo's* restaurants, as recommended by guide books and travel agents, as well as "decent" hotels near the city center, were all too costly. George and I decided to go south to the coast, too, with the difference that I talked him into hitchhiking.

With nightfall the Mexicans seemed to leave the city center while foreigners streamed in to occupy all the outdoor seating. They commenced drinking and waited in excellent view for some "National Geographic like" celebration, maybe a parade or dancing, "...with a lot of atmosphere," as one Brooklyn woman chimed. Soon, only artists and restaurant employees remained to represent the natives. The artists were trying to sell their paintings, rugs, carvings, and pottery. One annoyed and rich looking European declared, "Commercialism is ruining these people." All of the items for sale were excellent, but the visitors could have bought them anytime, and I didn't think that any visitors were in the mood to carry around an lot of souvenirs on Christmas Night; gifts for people back home could be bought right before leaving the country. There was about one artist for every tourist.

The waiters and waitresses seemed to be getting angrier all the time. I could sympathize with them. The tourists were from the richer countries of the world and represented a wide variety of languages and cultures. Many customers seemed to have little patience with restaurant personnel who couldn't speak eight or more languages, such as German, Italian, French, Japanese, Dutch, English, and a few from Scandinavia, plus Spanish, and serve them in the way they were accustomed. In my travel and work experience, only Canadians and people from the U.S. tip consistently; the inconsistency of the foreigners must have annoyed the Mexicans too. At about eight, as if on cue, the artists packed up and left, and waiters seemed to be harder to find. There had been no parade. The foreigners seemed to hang around and wonder what had just happened. Though this was the center of Oaxaca, I sensed that its heart was in the homes of the people. But we perpetual travelers built a few of our own places, and I was soon to find one.

The morning after, I exchanged money and repaid George. Then we went to the *mercado* for a great breakfast. From there, we shouldered our packs and walked to the south side of town to try our luck at hitching a ride to the coast, about three hundred kilometers and some seven hours away. A lot of cars sped by and we waited for an hour. Before giving up, and joining the other tourists, a man walked up to us and said that his cousin would drive by soon in his bus.

He would give us a ride to Pochutla, which is near the coast, and that it would cost only seven thousand pesos.

The narrow, rusted school bus came swaying down the road, swerved onto the soft shoulder almost running George and I over and skidded to a halt in a cloud of dust. With a smile from the driver we clambered on and sailed away. George moved toward the back of the bus and found a comfortable place to stand. He was near the only others on the bus who spoke English, Felipe and Pepe of Ciudad de México. I stayed up front and sat on my pack in the aisle. Way ahead was the Sierra Madre del Sur, a range that we would have to climb before descending to the coast. Despite the feverish speed at which the bus traveled, it took a long time to get to the base of the mountains. The pavement narrowed to two lanes with no shoulders. In each of the towns, speed bumps slowed the bus. In some communities, to get to bus stops, the bus drove down dirt side streets between close brick walls, the chuckholes swallowed tires, and dogs and roosters scrambled to get out of the way. At the bus stops, vendors came aboard and squeezed down the aisle to loudly announce the plates of food they offered, while other sellers worked the open windows of the bus. Then suddenly, the bus would peel out and the little vendors would plow with the force of offensive linemen to get to the door and jump off.

On a particularly long stretch of open road, wondering how the mountains would be if the Oaxaca Plateau was so rough, I looked up to the ceiling and along the walls over the rows of windows. Above there were paintings of saints, angels, and a pearly gate. Suspended rosaries and medallions swayed, flowers in vases were duct taped to the walls, and beautiful calligraphy on cards, that I presumed to be prayers, were taped everywhere. Although I am not religious, I thought, "We're gonna need them."

The road started abruptly off the plain, the switchbacks on that highway are more numerous than in all of Colorado. Some cars couldn't handle the strain and pulled off the road. When breakdowns occurred around blind curves, the passengers set warnings by putting branches on the pavement a hundred meters in each direction from their vehicle. Surprisingly, our bus didn't strain a bit. Luckily there was little traffic on that part of the road. Although I was both impressed and intimidated, the driver went as fast as he could as he listened to, and sometimes sang along with, loud *Latino* tapes, laughing wildly when he was tickled by the lady behind him. The only time that everyone became sober was when we passed white painted crosses. These often had rosaries draped on them and plastic flowers at their base. They were where others had driven for the last time. Everyone crossed themselves as we passed.

On top of the range the air was cool and fog rolled through the pines. Large areas of steep hillside had been cleared. As we descended the steep road the temperature rose and the vines and broad leaved vegetation more closely resembled a jungle. We arrived in Pochutla well after dark. George had gotten to know Pepe and Felipe. They knew of a sort of "hammock hotel" on a hillside overlooking a beach. They invited us along. The four of us went by taxi until the road was impassible. From there we walked through a palm grove to the wet sand at the surf's edge. The night was very black, but the pounding Pacific and strong warm breeze were sensational, I was excited to see what it looked like during the day. Bars and hammock hotels were off to the top of the strand. According to Pepe, just two years before, none of these businesses were here.

At the dark end of the beach was a rocky promontory protecting the hillside that our place was on. Makeshift kerosine jar lanterns were on each of the broad log and dirt steps. The sign read "Shambhala," and we were greeted by a statue of Buddha.

III.
On the Coast

Shambhala turned out to be a "Buddhist/Spiritualist ecological resort." Although several of the employees and guests were Buddhists, no pressure was ever put on anyone to convert to their beliefs. The clientele was about half Mexican and the rest European, Aussies and Kiwis, Canadian, some from the States, and others. Most of the buildings were simple frames with palm-thatch roofs and no walls; *palapas*. The hammocks were suspended from the wooden skeleton. I feared that hammocks would offer too much of a curve to sleep on, but others showed us how to lay in them. Simply unfold, sit at a right angle to its length, do a sixty degree pivot as you lean back, put your feet on the edge and push away to spread it and settle perfectly flat. A rope from a beam above could be tugged to make a well balanced hammock rock. I had a sleeping bag and so it was not too tough. George only had a blanket and had to awkwardly wrap himself in it. He landed on the sandy floor first try. Once settled, it turned out to be the most comfortable bed I had ever slept in. Our *palapa* slept about a dozen people.

Enjoying a cup of *té negro* (black tea), on the patio of the establishment's cliff-side semi-vegetarian restaurant (fish and chicken sometimes available), I had an excellent view of one of México's few nude beaches. Playa Zipolite, Zapotec for "the killer beach," is so named for the strong undertows that have taken many lives. From rocky headland to headland the sand stretched for about three kilometers (two miles). The sand strip was set back from the two rough peninsulas in a gentle crescent. During low tide the beach was up to two hundred meters wide, but only about fifty at high tide. At the upper edge of the beach were, between palm trees, *palapa* sheltered inns, bars and restaurants. A few years ago Zipolite only had Shambhala for tourists to stay in.

George had to go to Puerto Angel, an hour and a half walk, to get some things in the stores there. I would have gone with him, but, as is his custom, he was up at first light. I went for a swim in the powerful waves. There were two woman that wore 1930's looking beige wrap around hats. By their sun headgear I would have thought they were old-maid librarians. However, they were in their twenty's and naked. Our hammocks were in the same *palapa*, and so I had something to start a conversation with. They were Kathrin and Dagmar of Germany. The three of us sunned and swam together. When George came back, I was kind enough to introduce him to the women. That evening we ate together and went up to the highest point at Shambhala -the meditation center. It was about thirty meters (one hundred feet) above the crashing waters, and the furthest southern point in México until the Soconousco Coast. There we watched the brilliant red ball of the sun be extinguished by the Pacific. Many others gathered around too, and this was repeated nightly, some in yoga positions, while the rest sat talking quietly.

Up until three years ago there had been a building at the meditation center. One night the place mysteriously caught fire and a big fat laughing Buddha was pushed over the cliff. As Pepe sighed, "That's no way to treat a Buddha." All that remained was a whitewashed plaster wall built against a mound. It had niches and shelves and a fireplace carved into it. Formerly the wall was decorated with vases of flowers, sea shells and pretty stones, religious paintings, candles and holy books, as it would again be on the eve of the new year. Above the wall and on the cliff's edge had been Gloria's bedroom, she was founder and owner of Shambhala. In front of the wall there had been an altar, as well as a lending library open to guests and the local Zapotecs.

Gloria had been a 1960's and 70's Vietnam War protester in the United States. At some point she started wandering around México and was attracted to where the meditation center is now. Then, eighteen years before, Zipolite was accessible only by trail or boat. A dense forest with a wild assortment of cacti, vines, brush and trees occupied the area. Though she got scratched up badly, she was magnetically pulled to the farthest point, where she would soon build her bedroom. She could not back away as the place was so "powerful." She looked out as the sun set and cried. She stayed there until the sun rose out of the ocean in the east.

Though the Zapotec *ejidaderos* (people that live on *ejidos* -common land similar to Indian reservations in the U.S.), thought Gloria was a crazy *gringa*, they have come to respect her as she had helped the people in negotiations with the developers which were coming in, primarily from Ciudad de México, to build up the beach front. In addition, she hired the locals and used them in all the hotel positions. The Zapotecs had never had any work experience outside of subsistence farming and fishing, supplemented by a little work on nearby coconut plantations, sugar and banana company harvesting, and coffee plantations against the mountains. Training such people for work so radically different from what they were used to was a formidable task. In few of Zipolite's new businesses were the dark Zapotecs working at much more than cleaning toilets and raking the sand floors. In fact, they were rather unfriendly and jaded in

Zipolite. If Zipolite were to follow the pattern set in other coastal resorts, *palapas* would be followed by concrete hotels.

On the twenty-eighth in Shambhala, excitement was brewing as preparations for the new year celebration were getting under way. Carlos Luis, the "general manager," was jumping up and down in his bare feet and baggy white cottons, inviting people to help prepare the meditation center, and to go there in the evenings to practice mantras. I helped build a railing to keep people from going the way the big fat laughing Buddha had gone. The sun and wind were so desiccating that I couldn't work for long, since Shambhala had run out of water that day. In recent years, water often had to be delivered by truck, as wells were going dry or becoming saline. This is due to the recent demand for fresh water placed on the aquifer by new development.

As I settled into my hammock until water arrived, I was already feeling like a beach veteran. New arrivals could be spotted as they were invariably tired, cranky, stiff, and as they looked at Shambhala, seemed to be saying to themselves, "I guess I haven't seen everything yet." Sitting on a hammock near to me was a dejected looking Anglo woman in her early twenties. She was from Los Angeles. I asked her what was wrong. She said she had somehow become separated from her friends, and as it was the busy vacation season, there was nothing to rent but a hammock in this *"end-of-the-beach spiritual center."* I suggested that she try to relax, that she would soon get used to the people milling in and out of our open-air dormitory. She said she couldn't. She didn't. The next day she returned with a cabby to carry her suitcase a kilometer down the beach to the ticking meter. Apparently, she had found a room the night before after trying really hard. Shambhala is not a place for the material-territorialist.

I had the chance to talk to Gloria. She is a short, chubby, energetic fifty-two year old woman. She explained that it was no accident that she was drawn to this place:

> "A long time ago, where the Gobi Desert is today, there was a place where all the people lived in peace in a beautiful paradise. It was called Shambhala. It's neighbors grew militant and very strong. They fought vicious battles amongst themselves for control of Shambhala. The people at Shambhala did not want to be conquered by anyone. They were disgusted with the greed of their neighbors. So, rather than be captured, they took a vote and decided to ask God to destroy them.
>
> "When the destruction came Shambhala was pushed so far into the ground, and the impact was so great, that the Himalaya Mountains were uplifted. The rumble destroyed all Earthly countries and technological knowledge -things that we have since redeveloped. The energy going out from Shambhala was so great that it connected up with the electrical currents on the ocean floor that connect all major peninsulas."

People all over the globe, in little groups -some apparently inland- would perform similar ceremonies on New Years Eve, and again on an even more important date, January 11, 1992. The latter date has to do with a convergence to mark the end of one period of time and the beginning of another. The period would be the end of ten two thousand year eras. Some major changes would occur on Earth; these Buddhists always have an excuse to celebrate.

Gloria planed to retire in the next two years and give the business to the Zapotec employees. She worried as a few years earlier Club Med had tried to get hold of Shambhala. She vowed to stay on only as an advisor to the Zapotecs.

Each day at Shambhala seemed to float backwards

and forwards to the next. I laid in the hammock a lot, went swimming with my friends, and didn't really want to leave because I wanted to see if our railing would hold up when the crowd came for the celebration.

That day I spoke with Carlos Luis. He was in his mid thirties and originally from Ciudad de México. He had been around the world working as an interpreter and chef. For the previous six months he had been at Shambhala and seemed very happy. There he could avoid the thing he hated most in the world -money. Shambhala provided him room and board, and if he needed something Gloria would buy it for him. In addition, there was plenty of good marijuana in the area. Of this he added, "I just have to take care that Gloria does not see any pot; she doesn't want Shambhala to get closed down. I get high five to seven times a day," though he complained, "But I work all the time ...it's too much ...all the time...."

I met Harvey of Vancouver Island. He was in his early forties. It was his third winter visit to Shambhala. At the celebration he would have the honor and responsibility of being the "bellman." Between mantras he would ring a hand held bell and sing aloud the next mantra so that beginners would know what to say. He was an interesting character who couldn't find answers in either alcohol or bridge construction for the timber industry in the Canadian north. In 1992, financially secure, he enjoyed kayaking on the Strait of Georgia, mountain biking, and light carpentry. In the winter he likes to go to México since it is warm and not rainy, it's affordable, Shambhala attracts interesting people, and, "it has a good view."

Off and on I spoke to Mateo (Mat) of New Jersey. He had been at Shambhala for sixteen weeks; "Sure beats Jersey." He sometimes jumped in to help when the kitchen was overburdened. That gave him a special status and purpose at Shambhala. He was getting sick of the Zipolite scene, though, and I could see why in a buddy of his; Samuel of Cornwall.

Tall and in his early twenties, Samuel was obviously not taking care of himself. He was nearly skin and bone, and was "saving on food to invest in drugs." Once, when I couldn't figure out what he was saying, he exclaimed, "Sorry, sometimes I don't know what I'm saying!" I felt that he couldn't go on much longer before a British consulate agent would have to scoop him off the beach and place him on a London bound plane. Zipolite is full of Samuels.

Finally, the big day came and people where busily topping off the kerosine lamps, sweeping the trails through Shambhala with brooms made of branches tied together, and decorating the wall and the rest of the meditation center. The celebration was for the good that had happened in the past year, as well as a dashing off of negative energy, a cleansing, and a base upon which to build a good new year.

Toward evening, people flowed toward our end of the beach. Close to three hundred people crowded onto the meditation point. They stood behind the seven in white gowns, including Gloria and Dagmar, with their backs to the new railing. All faced west to chant as the sun set. Then the ones in gowns turned to pass through the crowd to the flower, herb and candle encircled area where they would perform rites appropriate to a new year. Most people held incense sticks or candles, and every third person held pages with the mantras. Several people wore flowered necklaces and crowns. There was no need for anyone to ask for silence. Harvey rang the bell three times and pronounced the first mantra out loud. The seven in gowns moved inward and backed away from the bare two meter pole that the flowers would be tied to. As they did this they chanted mantras and performed a dance that they had practiced for several days. Most of the people in the crowd swayed and chanted too. Nevertheless, to many people this scene was foreign and therefore scary. Some people stood back and showed fear in their faces, as though the next activity would be throwing a virgin over the cliff. I wasn't worried about that, by now I was confidant that nothing could get past the new railing.

The event was cheerful, and in fact it reminded me of Catholic Christmas parties. I had no idea what the chants meant, and doubted that more than a dozen people knew, but I took them as harmless. One of the tongue twisting chants, *"Cantos a Dios"* (Song to God) went, for example:

> u...u...namu...guru devdi namu,
> na... a mu namu, guru devdi...namu
> na...amu...na...a...mu...guru...
> de...e...devdi...na...a...mu.
> gopa la....gopa la....
> de paki nanda ne....gopa la

etcetera. The rhythm was not unlike "Jingle Bells," which was not surprising, considering that the essence of many celebrations around the world are similar.

After thirty minutes the ones in gowns threw flowers and splashed spring water from the mountains on everyone. Then the seven tied a few bundles of flowers to the pole and invited everyone to do the same. It was chaotic but fun, everyone who wanted to participate could. The pole, dense with flowers, and somehow resembling a Christmas tree, was laid horizontal and carried by two tall Germans along the winding path down toward the central part of Shambhala. Everyone danced and sang out simple chants as the procession moved slowly along. Flowers that couldn't be tied to the pole, for there were too many, or that fell, were picked up by those that followed. We went by the restaurant and down to the beach, past the welcoming Buddha, and onto the sand to a bonfire. The line of people followed the pole carriers as they proceeded in a wide circle around the fire. After a couple of times around, the decorated post was thrown into the flames, and everyone with flowers in their hands did the same. In that way the flowers had absorbed everyone's accumulated bad vibes from the year before and they were consumed.

The largest bottle rockets I had ever seen were randomly handed out. They flew high into the air and set off deafening explosions. In addition, Gloria had prepared a big table of food so that people would not only start off the new year having had a good time, but also with a full stomach. Samuel had some much needed nourishment and became more lucid. I thought that the concepts in the celebration -not to mention the food,- might entice him to get his life on a healthier track.

George showed his British half and avoided the event in exchange for swinging in his hammock and reading a science fiction novel by candle light. He later accused Dagmar of being *"superstitious."* She retorted, "You're *scientific!"* Their tiff was unfortunate since they had started to look like a promising couple. Miraculously, they patched up their differences over the next few days.

As George and Dagmar had been busy with each other in the days before the New Year, Kathrin and I had become close. That night she had gone to the festivities with me, but decided that it wasn't for her when the chanting started. She joined me later on the beach when the dozen remaining folks were sitting around the fire listening to someone play the guitar. The less chaotic scene was more familiar to her.

The next day Kathrin, Dagmar, Harvey, and myself took a walk westward along the coast. Behind Shambhala we entered an almost leafless forest; during the dry season the vegetation sheds leaves that there is no water for. The paths were familiar to Harvey as he had been there before. Our first stop was a little cove with calm water below towering rock walls. We all swam. The tide was low and we were able to walk around rocky headlands to a long, undeveloped beach, although there was what appeared to be a partly completed hotel that had been given up on several years prior. At one rocky point interrupting the beach was a cave that was tall enough to stand in, wide enough for a truck, and went back about thirty meters. It was sandy floored and would flood at high tide.

Walking on, we arrived at San Augustine, now only a collection of shacks and a restaurant under a flat topped palm roof with a sand floor. We stopped there for lunch and ordered chicken dinners. As we ate, live chickens protested their kin being eaten by pecking at our feet. Seaward, the low tide sands swept out to join craggy islets to the shore and formed embayments that made luxurious swimming lagoons. Walking on we came to the buildings that once provided a good living for the locals, a "sea turtle factory." Although it had been closed for three years, by an order from the Mexican government to protect endangered animals, a stench of death remained.

Suddenly, on cliffs, and in new territory for our Canadian guide, the women were wiser than Harvey and I and opted to go back a little ways to enjoy bathing in the sun and water. Between surging waves Harvey and I down climbed crab trodden rocks and held onto cracks in the cliff to keep from being washed away as the waves came in. Past these obstacles we arrived at Playa Mezunte. There the sharp crescent shaped beach is steep. Huge waves develop right near shore, rise high, then slam down on the gravelly slope as a torrent of water from the last wave rushes to the sea. This makes swimming a challenge, and dangerous. We walked to the end of the beach to where a rocky peninsula, Cabo Cometa, juts out to sea.

On the return we stopped to check out a new *palapa* operation and met the proprietors. They are Javier, Isabel, and their sons, Cristóbal, André, and Omar. I liked them and said that I would be back in a couple of days. Harvey and I found an inland road and followed it back to meet Dagmar and Kathrin.

On the third of January our little group broke up to go our separate ways. Kathrin and Dagmar caught a bus to San Cristóbal de las Casas, in Chiapas, an international travelers' center, and home of a university, sometimes called "The Boulder of México." George went back to Ciudad Oaxaca to see about a job teaching English. Harvey was to hang out at a quieter Shambhala for a few days. I headed back to Mezunte. I probably would have started for home immediately as my wad of money had become dangerously thin, but I was assured that traveling would be foolhardy until Monday, the sixth of January, as people would be returning to work from the holidays.

About one quarter of all Mexicans live and work in Ciudad de México, but they retain incredibly strong contact with their home villages. The capital is viewed as a place to make money, or to get an education. Consequently, when most people travel, it is not usually for a vacation in the sense that people from financially better off countries think of it, but rather a communion with family and old stomping grounds.

Although Ciudad de México is the world's largest city, with some twenty-five million people, it has only recently become such a large city. In 1950 it had 3,050,000, and by 1960 its population was still only 4,871,000; in 1970 it was the world's sixth largest city with 8,590,000 people. Many people in Ciudad de México, therefore, were not born there, and the children that are born in the city pick up their parents' identification with their home state, city or village. In this way, Ciudad de México, like most other Latin American capitals, becomes the center and heart of its nation. In México everyone refers to Ciudad de México as "México," leaving out the words *Ciudad de*. For variation it is sometimes called *La Capital*. In fact, it has been said that "In México, Ciudad de México *is* México."

The sum of all this would leave me stranded two thousand miles from my home in Colorado, and I would have to go through *La Capital* to get there. So I determined to at least make the best of the situation and try to enjoy my time as cheaply as possible. At Mezunte I paid only 5,000 pesos per night (versus 7,500 at Shambhala). The family running the place was nice, and the scenery is worth a million bucks. I took a long walk up a dry ravine inland from the coast. Some kid accosted me to kick around a soccer ball for a while. This we did for an hour. At each house I passed there seemed to be a dozen children. I felt obliged to return *"¡Hola!"* (Hello!) to each child lest one might feel left out. Their giggling was infectious. All the houses were surrounded by vegetable gardens and fruit trees, and animals, including chickens, goats, pigs, and mangy dogs. But not all was idyllic.

Of the dogs, they live a particularly harsh life. They

look very undernourished. Some are just skin, bones, and wounds. Many are no match for the average chicken. They sleep a lot and the flies bother them incessantly. Most sad of all, though, is that sometimes they are the victims of human outburst. I've seen children sneak up to sick sleeping dogs and start hitting them with a thick rope. The poor things run off yelping. They are certainly not the big dumb and spoiled dogs of the U.S. Somewhat more healthy feral dogs roam the beaches in packs. These have reportedly attacked people walking alone.

Using the creek bed as a path, a man and donkey passed hauling corn stocks. Two other men were cutting the same on a steep hillside. A trail diverged from the ravine and I followed it steeply upward. All was a thick though dry, leafless forest. Here and there, hacked out of the forest are burnt stump dotted corn fields.

Back at the *palapa* I met Victor Alvarez, a school teacher from Ciudad de México. We took a walk to the four room *escuela primaria*, a primary school. Only two rooms were in use, but the chairs and few desk looked very crowded. A lack of teachers, Victor surmised. On the outhouse door was a painting of Che Guevara, Argentine born Latin American Revolutionary and former right-hand man of Fidel Castro.

We went across the soccer field to the town square where a *tienda* (a small store) was open and the local kids were there playing the one Pacman video machine. Victor was annoyed that the kids were not at home studying. On the other side of the square several men were hanging around a pickup truck. They were passing bottles around and acting belligerent. One man fell backward and his bottle broke with a loud smash. Cursing and laughter erupted. Victor is a non drinker and very concerned about the problem of alcoholism, as well as the low funding level for education in his country.

At the *palapa* I met twenty year old Ingrid, an aspiring university student. She is from the capital and on vacation. She has been here for a couple of weeks and has come to know the family very well. The kids love her. She's obviously from a well-to-do Mexican family, being able to afford a real vacation, and has traveled to other places, too. Two years ago she spent a year traveling and working in Europe, mainly Germany, and likes Europe very much. She was nice to me, but she has a particularly harsh nationalistic side to her, as many wealthy Mexicans have. One time she went out of her way to change whatever we were talking about to let me know that she thought little of the United States, and although she had been there twice before, she thought that it offered nothing culturally and was quite boring. She would never waste her time going to the U.S. again.[5] She identified with Latin America and Europe for culture, particularly movies and music.

I didn't try to convince her otherwise; I simply found her comments amusing, and in light of U.S. interference in her country over the years, I could sympathize with her animosity. Perhaps she didn't mind talking to me, being from the U.S. and all, because I had read so extensively about her country and the rest of Latin America -an oddity for a U.S. citizen. Or perhaps it was just that stranded and penniless deep inside México, like many Mexicans illegally in the U.S., I was an easy target to vent steam upon.

---

[5]*This attitude is suspiciously European, as it seems to be in vogue with some Europeans. In México I've heard some Germans say to the effect: "I will not go to America [sic] because there is nothing to see there; Everything there is artificial, so I will not..."*

We took a walk through Mezunte to a newly cut road over a hill and descended to Playa Mermejita. The beach is a kilometer and a half long and no one lives there. The road was new. Ingrid told me that most of the locals hated it. They prefer small trails and do not want a lot of tourists scurrying around on this remote beach. It would be dangerous for swimmers anyway. Waves there form within ten meters of the shore. These are two meter tall, fast moving walls of water that crash onto the steep beach with bone breaking brutality. These are even worse than Mezunte's waves.

    We walked to the end of the beach where cliffs blocked our way. In a cave there were dozens of bats flying around. There was no litter or signs of humans on this beach. Then, suddenly, Juan popped up from a crevice. He held a net full of crabs. He explained that they were for his family and friends and invited Ingrid and I to visit him. He lived just passed the rocky cliffs on the next beach. I fancied him as a sort of Zapotec Henry David Thoreau; less the Harvard degree. He loves this wild beach and doesn't want it to become like Zipolite, with all its soldiers and tourists. Here he could swim nude, fish, dig for clams, catch oysters, and smoke marijuana. He has a nearby *rancho* (in this region, a small subsistence farm) and family. At that time his Canadian friend and *compadre* (godfather of his child) was visiting. He was emphatic that we go to his house sometime and enjoy his hospitality and the bounty of food that he could gather "in no time at all." His Spanish was especially unique, and Ingrid was translating for me, although I didn't quite get that the Canadian was visiting just then.

    We returned to the *palapa* at Mezunte and found that Harvey had just checked in. We told Harvey where we had gone and it was just where he wanted to go the next day, too, as he wanted to explore the beaches in that direction. Ingrid did not want to joint us though. Rather than taking roads inland, I suggested that we follow the rocky coast as close to the ocean as possible, even if it meant rock climbing. Harvey agreed.

Harvey had sailed passed this coast seventeen years prior on a trip from Kittery, Maine, to Vancouver Island via the Panama Canal, with a stop at Puerto Angel. He remembered this coast as especially wild and spectacular. We walked to where a cliff abutted the thinning width of the beach until it melted away and we were jumping along and climbing over rocks. When waves arrived we stood on top of big boulders in order not to be swept away. We came to a break in the cliff with a steep path that allowed us to scramble to higher ground. From there we could see Mezunte Bay's many palm trees, golden sand, and thatch roofed *palapas*.

Along the cliff edge trail we walked beneath three story cacti with arms locked in demented expression. Some brakes of brush looked impenetrable, while other areas were open and grassy. Soon the vegetation gave way to a veritable castle of wildly bent and contorted sandstone that looked like a frozen storm upon the sea. We scrambled up the rough landward side to look down into deep crevasses that filled and emptied with thousands of gallons of water.

The landward crevasses were protected from the full force of the waves, and when they drained we could see a soggy forest of seaweed alive with shells, snails and starfish, until the liquid curtain closed again. At the end of the natural fortress' ocean-battle-carved surface, we stood mesmerized gazing into a pounded-sterile chasm with the full speed and power of rollers arriving to fill it up instantly, then drain to only the wet rock below.

To proceed westward from this point, Cabo Cometa, we had to avoid a bay with waves pounding at the base of a cliff. We soon found ourselves way above the ocean in a thicket of nearly impenetrable brush. All the branches were twisted and knotted, and the trees were bent low between rocky ridges in the windy environment of the headland. There were many thorny bushes that scratched us, and their picky seeds attached themselves to our clothing. We each had a liter of water mixed with crushed vitamin C tablets and lime juice, a good tropical thirst squelcher. We needed every drop and more.

Finally we were able to descend to Playa Mermejita and retrace the route I took with Ingrid the day before. The cliff that had stopped Ingrid and I was obviously not impassible. All it took was clawing up vertical rock that hangs over pounding surf with stinging spray flying all over the place. From there you squeeze into a crack in the wall. The crack is at an oblique angle and points downward. By timing yourself to arrive at some wet boulders at the bottom of the crack between smashing waves, you shimmy on your chest face first, then, stand up and run to a large rock and climb it to avoid being crushed by a bulldozer of a wave. From there you have a little more beach to enjoy until the next cliff.

This was where it got interesting. The cliffs were bashed by powerful waves and there were no ledges or rocks at their base. To our right and landward, there was a steep, impenetrable thicket of vines, knotted brush, and snaking cacti. The pitch must have been 60 degrees or more, and could have only stood that steep because of an incredibly intricate root system. One narrow swath, however, had slid to reveal a strip of rocks and sand held in place by faith alone. This swath seemed to lead to the top of the cliffs. We climbed the hill using arms as much as legs. Each step up involved sliding back almost as much. Rocks kept tumbling down to the beach below, as did a steady slide of sand. All the debris would be washed away in the next storm.

    We reached the top, panting, and drank our last drops of water. Sea birds glided by on the breeze. Below, behind the waves in the clear water, a manta ray swam gently. Wind bent trees grew out of the cliff. It didn't look like we could go any further. But then Harvey noticed a slight ledge in the cliff, and though trees grew on it, these trees were leaning away from the cliff just enough, it looked, to get our bodies between them and the cliff. With nothing below us we stepped from tree trunk to tree trunk. After ten meters we emerged triumphantly onto a rocky point and could see the next beach down below us. It was an endless looking beach, and behind it was a coastal plain complete with marshes and lagoons. We started looking for a way to climb to the beach below. Fishermen on the beach sternly motioned us to go up the hill further into the dense forest. Below us was a dangerously high cliff. We took their advice and made our way over entangled cacti and vines. Deeper in the forest were tall tree sized cacti with vines hanging from them. I had always associated cacti with deserts and vines with jungles. Here, though, nature didn't care about my stereotypes. I couldn't imagine that Juan had regularly taken the route we had taken, and I was right. Eventually we came upon a small trail that made the going easier. The trail suddenly plunged down a steep embankment and we were soon on the right beach, and facing the largest and whitest albino Newfoundland dog I had ever seen. It must have weighed 80 kilograms (175 pounds.)

    In fear I almost turned to find some handy cactus to

climb. The furry dog only wagged its tail, though, and couldn't have chased me anyway, as it was sweating and panting profusely in the heat. A little blond girl came over and took the dog by the collar and walked it away. We followed and came to a couple of vans with Ontario plates. Here we found Juan's *compadre* sitting in a lawn chair. His wife and two daughters were there. His white, beer bellied brother was toying with a soccer ball. The brothers were originally from Hungary and departed with Soviet bullets following them. Now they were settled in northern Ontario. But Canadian winters are too cold, so they spend winters here on this wild shore. Juan was swinging in a hammock with a bottle of Canadian Whiskey. He had drool coming out the side of his mouth. He wasn't up for entertaining, let alone foraging for dinner. We filled our water bottles from their supply and inquired as to the road back to Mezunte. Darkness was not far off so we had to get going. By the time we got to Mezunte it was pitch black and we were thoroughly tired.

Big excitement hit Mezunte on the fifth. The governor of the state was coming to visit. Several soldiers lounged under the palm trees. I spoke to Stephen, the governor's driver. Stephen told me the gist of what was going on. In a year the coast road from Pochutla to San Antonio would be widened and paved and pass right through Mezunte near the square. A concrete hotel would replace all the *palapas*. Decent jobs would finally come to these people. Soon the governor would arrive for a press conference and town meeting.

I was somewhat taken aback, since I knew that tourist development ought to be planned with caution. I knew that I couldn't speak to the governor himself, so I hoped that by telling the governor's driver what I thought, he would relay to the governor what the crazy *gringo* with no money had said. It was my best hope. I pointed out to Stephen that the beach really wasn't suitable for swimming because of the brutal waves here, and that the people were already quite happy. If it were more like Zipolite, the people that are here now might be displaced or have to do menial jobs that would suspend them in poverty. I was too shocked to be very articulate. Several years of studying rural economics and reading John Nicoles' books had convinced me that resort development is a false panacea.

The dinning *palapa* was soon requisitioned by soldiers who placed all the tables in a row to make one long table and arranged the chairs around it. A film crew set up cameras at one end. The governor would sit at the opposite end. Javier stood back a respectable distance and looked on. The rest of us swung in our hammocks and waited for the governor. There was Ingrid, Harvey, William a U.C.L.A. student, and myself. The governor walked briskly down the road from the main square, past the school and onto the beach, then straight to the dinning *palapa* without ever looking at the surf. He made one glance in our direction, then he instinctively turned his head away in disgust. The whole village followed at his heals. Only the governor and soldiers wore shoes. The villagers didn't own any. While the villagers were listening intently in this atmosphere of great importance, we in the springing hammocks were mocking and laughing cynically about the governor and his development plans.

Javier hadn't moved during the whole event. He just looked on. He noticed the disrespectable attitudes we had toward the governor's plans, versus how monumental the governor's visit and plans were to the villagers. I wondered what was going on in his mind. Could he have known that he might soon be demoted from being a palapa proprietor to a seasonal hotel janitor -if he were lucky? What of his sons? Would they have the opportunity to live off the land and sea? Would the little fresh ground water available be muscled away from the community by a concrete hotel? What influences would they come into contact with? Were the schools preparing the kids to be successful in modern livelihoods? He probably presumed that we travelers were better educated than anyone living in Mezunte. One thing for sure, Javier is no dummy, I could tell that he perceived that Mezunte was facing complicated times.

With foreboding thoughts it was time for me to leave Mezunte. But I knew that I would be back someday, particularly if the area didn't change too much. I would hardly be able to bear seeing Mezunte's happy Zapotecs become jaded like Zipolite's.

IV.
A Journey Through History

Harvey walked with me the five kilometers to San Antonio. From there I took a local bus to Puerto Escondido. Unfortunately, there were no direct buses to either Ciudad Oaxaca or to the capital. However, I was assured that if I took a bus to Acapulco I would have a good chance of catching a bus to the capital.

A lady in the aisle had four babies. One slept on my lap, the baby in her arms slept with its head on my shoulder. Her pregnant stomach bobbed in front of my face. Although it was a direct bus we stopped a lot and made small detours. The bus broke down, but it was only forty minutes before another bus, already half full of people, came along and picked us up. There was a lot of grumbling as we rode on through the night. I stood in the aisle at the very front of the bus so that I could see what was going on. The bus slowed down for burrows and cattle along the way, but most of the time it was able to speed along on the narrow and shoulderless two lane highway. We arrived in Acapulco at 1:00 A.M. The station was crowded. There wouldn't be seats available on buses to the capital until 4:00 P.M. I shrugged and bought a ticket. Although all the theories I had heard assured me that on Monday, January 6, traveling would be no problem as everyone would be settled back at work or school, I had obviously run into the stragglers. I dubbed this day "Saint Monday."

I was now down to only 200,000 pesos (approximately $70.00); thus, although the shower felt great, the 60,000 peso hotel room really hurt. In the morning, at a breakfast counter, I ordered some chicken and cheese *flautas*. They were pulled out of a freezer and factory wrapped. They were zapped in a micro wave. After eating them I slowly started to feel cramps. I ignored these, as I usually do with sickness, and ninety-nine percent of the time whatever is bothering me goes away.

Like the station, the bus was as new and clean as any I had seen anywhere. We passed a tollbooth and barreled along on an *autobahn* quality highway. From high above the city I could take in a view of Acapulco's harbor. At the base of these mountains is enclosed the deep-water port, the best natural harbor in México. In the early colonial era (the sixteenth century) there was only a seasonally occupied cluster of buildings here, where the Manila Galleons were received and sent out. "Spanish Silver" was exported to the Orient, and silk, porcelain, tea, and spices came back.[6] Today, with almost half a million inhabitants, almost all poor, and a world famous jet-setters's destination, it's a city with a unique blend of problems. In the alleys, which seem to double as sewers, there are pigs rolling that will make their way to dinner tables. In the harbor float luxury liners, oil tankers, and cargo ships. I can see how it used to be a tropical paradise, but today it's a dump. Only the transportation corridors are kept up, allowing travelers to avoid seeing too much of México's urban poverty.

After twenty miles the modern road detoured onto an older road and through the *campesino* villages of rural Guerrero and Morelos. The new road was often seen under construction many miles away. It consists of the deepest road

---

[6]*For further description, including that of these great voyages, see Francesco Caretti's* My Voyage Around the World, *translated by Herbert Weinstock. New York: Random House, Inc., 1964.*

cuts I had ever seen, and whole valleys that were filled in to make the future road level.

In this rugged country, during the Mexican Revolution of 1910 to 1920, guerrilla armies of poorly equipped *campesinos,* under the command of macho folk generals whose authority rested upon the strength of their character, such as Emiliano Zapata, swept back and forth over the land chasing and retreating from well armed government troops. These were sent to protect the investments of great land owners. These wealthy people, usually resident in Ciudad de México, had investment money and mechanical means, namely a railroad, to exploit whatever the land could produce, such as timber and sugar. They also had the legal power to take possession of untitled land, though it had been used by generations of *campesino* corn and bean subsistence farmers.[7]

By taking the lands of *campesinos*, who could rarely provide proof of legal ownership, the poor were reduced to dependence and peonage. But they fought back for the right to return to a subsistence life style. Immediately after the war it appeared that the *campesinos* had won. However, different reasons caused mass migrations of people to the capital, other cities, and to the U.S. As will be related below, today's Central American revolutions, along with the rapid growth of capital cities, and the emigration of many people to the U.S., bears resemblance to the sequence of events that occurred here.

In the night the bus crested one last hill and a molten caldera of lights appeared below. It was the capital.

---

[7]*Note that the turmoil and its causes that erupted in the state of Chiapas, January 1, 1994, almost perfectly mirrors these earlier events.*

The lights more or less demarcate the floor of the great inter mountain basin that once held Lake Texcoco, now mostly drained. Long before Europeans came here, in the lake was a low rocky island that none of the established kingdoms were interested in. Here a vicious and barbaric group of wandering misfits settled, because their gods told them to, and because they were not welcome anywhere else. They were hired as mercenaries in war; their most notable talent was fighting. They built a city called Tenochtitlán, and they eventually dominated the whole basin. These were the Aztec. Their city had a population of over 100,000 by the early sixteenth century, making it one of the world's largest cities at that time. For that time, the basin's population has been estimated at anywhere from four and a half million to twenty million people, all either allies or servants of the ferocious Aztecs on their island in Lake Texcoco.

At Templo Mayor, near today's National Cathedral, the hearts of living captured warriors were cut out with obsidian knives. The bodies were then pushed down the steep steps of the pyramid. Their bodies were eaten ceremonially, and their heads were put on display on nearby racks containing tens of thousands of skulls. But the Aztec nobility and high priests saw this act as necessary: Without the sacrifice of the hearts of captured warriors, the sun would not rise, since it would not be well enough nourished to continue its battle with the night. This need for prisoners to sacrifice necessitated the perpetuation of war. Needless to say this caused the Aztecs to accumulate a large number of enemies. In some years in the second decade of the sixteenth century, it is estimated that over ten thousand warriors were sacrificed. Then from the east came great houses upon the sea, the Spanish ships of Hernán Cortes.

It was 1519. Without wasting a moment, Cortes assessed the situation and threw himself behind and directed the opposition to the Aztecs. At first there were only five hundred Spaniards with him. Another thousand joined him later. Without Indian allies, however, he could have never conquered Tenochtitlán. Cortes' political shrewdness and mechanical ingenuity, including the construction of large boats with cannons mounted on them, prevailed over the Aztecs in one of history's greatest battles which lasted for over two years.

In the end the Spaniards didn't change the agriculturally orientated, tribute paying Indians' society much. Instead, what they did was replace the Aztec royalty and nobility with themselves. This explains much of today's Latin American power structure: Indians are usually at the bottom of the social, political, and financial ladder, while pure blood Spaniards are usually at the top. In between are the Mestizos, or mixed blooded people, who, at least in the case of México, are the majority of the population today. One aspect of the Mexican Revolution was to try and change the power hierarchy and to bring about a degree of equality. The theory of *"Raza Cósmica"* (Cosmic Race) was developed, stating that a fifth great human race[8] was evolving in México, and it was a blend of Indian and Spanish. Most Mexicans know the stories I have told, and they are fiercely proud of their history. In the capital I was soon to see some tangible results of this pride.

The bus stopped at Topo, which serves buses going to all southern and eastern México. The place is like an airport,

---

[8]*The others are the familiar Caucasian, Negro, Mongoloid, and American Indian*

complete with concourses, gate areas, restaurants, and it was swarming with people. I definitely needed help getting to the train station. A police officer directed me to the metro. Two metro employees then led me to a map of the metro and sent me in the right direction. Obviously looking lost, a Mexican drew me a map with directions from the "Revolución" metro stop to the train station. At 1:00 A.M. I was outside the locked front doors of the train station. All was pitch black.

I was not cheerful. Here I was in the world's largest city and alone in the dark. I knew for sure that some gang would kill me before sunup. Then they came at me. They were at least a dozen. "Is it ready?" asked a man with a burly Highlands' accent and wearing Scottish tweeds.

"Excuse me?"

"The train?"

"I hope so."

Another man went to the door and discovered that it was locked. From inside a security guard ran to the door and opened it. The well dressed group of a dozen Brits, Europeans, and North Americans entered the station with authority. Not to be outclassed I shouldered my pack and followed.

At the loading dock was an engine with a single car attached. Here I thought I'd better stop. They disappeared into their little train and it pulled away immediately. I was left standing there not knowing quite what to do. At least now I was in the building and off the street. I went and asked the security guard if it was O.K. for me to be in the building. He didn't care one way or the other. With him I went on his rounds and we talked for a good two hours. We went to the station's lower level where street people, and poor people waiting for trains, were allowed to sleep. These people looked like they had just gone through a nuclear war. In the main lobby I slept for a couple of hours beside the security guard's desk.

In the morning I bought my ticket, but the train would not be leaving until 8:00 P.M. I left my pack in pay storage. I took a bus down Avenida Insurrección to Ciudad Universitaria, the Western Hemisphere's largest university. It has over 327,000 students. The 1968 Summer Olympics were held here, and the main stadium is across Insurgentes from the Jardín Central (Central Garden) of the university. The school is, as the nickname implies, a city all its own. México has been called a country of murals, and the world's largest are located here. Juan O' Gorman, in 1952, transformed the fifteen story Biblioteca (Library) into a visual textbook depicting the historical experience of México. The mural is made out of millions of tiny rocks of differing colors. David Siqueriros' masterpiece on the administration building depicts the labor of the nation supporting the students, whom in turn, return their skills for the betterment of the nation.

One aspect of the <u>Mexican Revolution</u> was an inward look for inspiration in art. Previous to the <u>Mexican Revolution</u>, all of Latin America looked toward Europe for artistic inspiration, all native art forms were looked down upon as being innately inferior. However, the <u>Mexican Revolution</u> took the bold step of celebrating the Indian past of the nation, creating the "Indianist" movement, thus fostering a special pride, or nationalism, in México. The murals of Ciudad Universitaria, and on other buildings in the capital, are done in a stylized Aztec fashion, and the likes of these can only be found in México. I literally spent two hours studying the murals of the Biblioteca.[9] But there is plenty of European art left over from prior to the revolution, in several museums. Besides the revolutionary art, the university has a reputation for being a center of political protest.

In 1968, just a few days before the Summer Olympics were to open, a student protest was put down brutally and many were killed. The government now admits its troops killed about thirty "armed communists." Students, such as Pepe and Felipe, that I met at Zipolite, insist that between twelve to fifteen thousand unarmed students and professors were killed. Even if the truth is 25% higher than what the government admits, and 75% less than Pepe and Felipe claim, the numbers are staggering. We do know that several hundred people were incarcerated until 1970. What is really amazing is that the incident was completely covered up, even in the foreign press until well after the Olympic Games were over. The 1988 Seoul, South Korea student protests are said to be analogous to the 1968 protest here, where students seem to have planned to use the large foreign press that would become available during the Olympic Games to press their government toward needed reforms.

Victor had given me his number and told me to give him a call when I was passing through the capital, after 4:00, when he would be off work at the school. This I did and he came to pick me up in his mother's car. I didn't have much time before my train left, so he gave me a tour of some parts of the city that one must see. We drove down the wide Paseo

---

[9]*For a good guide to the symbolism in the murals, and art at the university, see* Let's Go Mexico. *My version is from 1985, it is written by the Harvard Student Agencies, Inc., St. Martin's Press, New York. pp. 116-18.*

de la Reforma with its many monuments that grace ornate traffic circles, making this avenue one of the most beautiful in the world. We passed the great, pure white Palacio de las Bellas Artes (Palace of Fine Arts), a decidedly European structure, and as beautiful as any building I have seen in Europe.

In dangerous counterpoint to all this were the "windshield washers." These were usually young kids that ran out to cars at traffic lights. They sprayed car windshields and wiped off the spray with dirty rags. If you did not tip them for "washing your windshield," it could result in a dent kicked into the car or a long scratch along the car made with a metal object. I was a little concerned about the kids and asked Victor if they are ever hit by cars in their desperate quest for money. Victor regretfully replied, "Regularly." In addition to this, the traffic was the most mind boggling that I have seen anywhere. I have driven in Boston, the proud holder of the United States' highest auto-accident insurance rates, and Ciudad de México is worse.

All too soon, though, it was approaching the time to depart. To Victor it was a pity that I could not see more of his city, and I had to agree, but I knew that I would be back. Usually I have an allergic reaction to the mere thought of cities; I travel the back paths of society. Yet here I was in the world's largest city and wanting to linger. Back in Colorado, school would recommence soon, and I wasn't rich enough to stick around anyway. Ciudad de México is no Mezunte where one can idle in a hammock, play soccer, and go on relaxing walks. Here was a city and in a city one needs money.

Victor walked me into the train station. He was glad to see me but said that I looked terribly sick. He was right. He invited me to return anytime and stay longer to experience more of the city, and to stay with him at his parents' house. The idea sounded great, and I would take him up on the offer in a year's time. For now though, I had to get back to my own world as best that I could.

Happily, the train north, the same route that I had taken south a few weeks earlier, proved much more comfortable. I had two padded seats to myself. The car and bathrooms were cleaner, the suspension was fine, the overhead light worked, and we made fewer stops and moved quicker. When I had traveled this route previously, being nearly Christmas, it was during the peak period of travel. Now the rush was over. It could be that the train I was on previously was pulled into service just for the holiday rush. In fact I'm sure this is the case, because then there were two trains traveling the route, whereas usually there is only one, and a good one at that.

At daybreak we were in Auguascalientes. The train passed over hilly country to the famous silver mining city of Zacatecas at 2,500 meters (8,000 feet) above sea level. From there the track descends imperceptibly, except for increasingly desert like conditions, onto the Central Mexican Altiplano. In this bleak country, during the sixteenth and seventeenth centuries, the Spanish and the nomadic Chichimecas waged war for one hundred and fifty years. The character of the natural environment and history here are very different from the south. Here, the population was not dense in the past; even now people live in concentrated areas, leaving the bulk of the country empty. Along the east and west mountainous borders of the Altiplano were located the silver mines that once made México the world's biggest producer of the metal. On the land between the mountains huge herds of cattle roamed freely and were there for the taking. *Vaqueros*, or cowboys, rode out to lasso them.

With the construction of the railroads, in the late eighteen hundreds, the land of the Altiplano became valuable, and was thus divided into ranch holdings, owned by Mexicans in the capital, and foreigners, so that the wealth of cattle could be exported to distant locations. Thus, *vaqueros*, reticent to change, were labeled *bandidos*, or bandits. Partly for this reason, then, the Mexican Revolution developed a northern counterpart to that of the south, where Zapata was active in Morelos, Guerrero, and Puebla.

Here in the north the area involved in military conflict was much larger, and the armies in revolt were far more modern; for instance, General Francisco "Pancho" Villa's "Army of the North" had its own hospital train, and his infantry moved about by train. Villa's shock troops consisted of cavalries that numbered in the thousands of men. Huge battles were fought on horseback until 1915, the year federalist forces were armed with German machine guns and barbed wire. Here the Germans perfected a strategy that devastated the cavalries and infantry units of their enemies in World War I. Giant **V**'s were formed with barbed wire; the cavalries were funneled into them, and a machine gun rattled at the small end into the charging horses.

Prior to this, although Villa and Zapata met and actually ruled México for a time from the capital itself, their government was not recognized by the U.S., and U.S. support (i.e., loans and arms), instead went to others, described below. Besides this, there were other weaknesses in the new government. The rationales for fighting were different. In the south it was about land reform. In the north it was about economic and political rights. Besides, Zapata never trusted Villa. The two were only united by a common dispossession at the hands of rapid modernization.

In México, too much modernization had taken place too quickly from 1876 to 1911, a period known as the "Porferiato," named after dictator Porfirio Díaz. Millions became landless and jobless in the quest to centralize the ownership of cultivable land in the south, and to exploit cattle in the north. Díaz stayed in power as long as he did because of his modern army.

Without Díaz there was left a power vacuum, for which no effective democratic mechanism existed to fill the gap. So who were Zapata and Villa fighting? They were fighting the "modernist" Venustiano Carranza and General Alvaro Obregón, who subsequently fought each other, with the latter beating out the former and becoming president in 1920. However, these modernists were different than Díaz. They had implicitly socialistic goals, along with, like Díaz, some fascist ideas. This group eventually evolved into the P.R.I., México's single political party with extensive power, and her nearly complete inheritance to this day. Although they did many things to enhance México's material situation, such as land redistribution and land reclamation, and they spread education and health care, it seems that the one party system allowed for a bureaucracy to become entrenched, which in turn became hopelessly inefficient, corrupt, secure, and oppressive. To this end they even reined in the religions, especially affecting the Catholic Church, with the following laws, and not repealed until 1992: Religious ceremonies were not to be held outside of a church; churches could not own land; churches were removed from primary and secondary education; members of the clergy were not allowed to criticize laws or to vote. This was to centralize popular control along modern political lines.[10]

---

[10]Camp, Politics in Mexico, 1993, chapter nine.

Today México seems to be experiencing a new burst of energy. It's economic outlook is promising, and problems such as the exploding birth rate are slowing down (in 1960 the birthrate was 3.6 per year, by 1985 it was down to 2.5). There is more political openness today than anyone would have dreamt of ten years ago. The elections of 1988 were ground breaking in that the P.A.N. won one governorship, that of Baja California, and several municipalities; also, other political parties did better than ever. This is probably due to fairer vote counting, which in turn is encouraging more Mexicans to participate in politics.[11]

There have been times when the one party state's oppression has generated violence, such as during the Cristero Revolt of the late 1920s and 1930s, principally in the west of the country. National violence almost erupted with the repression shown just prior to the 1968 Olympic Games, too. However, poverty and malnourishment are problems that are worsening, environmental degradation and the loss of frontier areas, or wilderness, are limiting traditional escape valves for the landless poor. Another traditional escape valve, immigration to the U.S., is always opening and closing and never certain. The scale of this human movement is huge, one in three Mexicans have been to the U.S.[12]

A country like this is always on the brink of war;[13] as are many of Central America's countries, as I shall relate

---

[11]*Ibid.*

[12]*Los Angeles Times* poll, August 1989, in Camp's *Politics in Mexico*, (Oxford U.P., 1993) 45.

[13]*According to Camp, in* Politics in Mexico, *this belief is widespread; a 1986 survey found that 50 percent of Mexicans thought that a revolution could occur within five years. Not withstanding the Chiapas rebellion of 1994, President Carlos Salinas, elected in 1988, seems to have been able to mollify the country.*

below. It's said that the only thing holding México together today is the historical memory of the revolution, when possibly three million of the country's then eighteen million people died. In light of today's new and "improved" ways of killing people, through more "advanced" military technology, the caution of the Mexicans is understandable.

Two large men in cowboy clothing, wielding guitars, entered the train in a cattle town. With deep voices they sang the folk songs of the Altiplano. I could not make out every word, but I did hear the name "Pancho Villa" sung in a voice that showed longing for his return and guidance. The train chugged along into the dawn, and in the distance riding over a low ridge in the Altiplano I saw a sight often reported in México; the ghost riders of the revolution galloping and shouting and shooting into the air, then disappearing into the setting sun. In Morelos Zapata is sometimes spotted. Although Villa and Zapata were both assassinated by the powers that came to dominate the country, their spirits live on, and Mexicans live on, poor in body but rich in soul.

We pulled into Ciudad Juarez at 7:00 A.M. I was so sick I could barely even walk. I had $5.00. I stood there hitching on an interstate highway ramp in El Paso. Everything was clean. All was efficient. Several shinny new cars with only one person inside drove by. The drivers only looked at me out of the sides of their eyes. They must of thought that I was a killer. Poor at least. I hadn't felt so out of place in a long time. I was warned to expect culture shock upon return to my own country, but I expected it to be a pleasant experience.

A yellow rusted pickup playing loud Latino music, sporting plates from the state of Sonora, with three guys in the front and a load of bananas in the back, swerved onto the ramp and skidded to a halt. I rode with the fruit. El Paso, and México across the Río Bravo, rolled back into the distance as we sped up Interstate 25. Near Las Cruces we pulled into a truck stop. Immediately the driver asked if I would like a cup of coffee. I said I would. They also bought me an order of toast. They would have bought me anything off the menu, but toast was all that I felt I could handle.

    I made it back to my apartment that night, thanks to the communal spirit of three rides after the one mentioned above. My pockets were bulging with four dollars. In the morning my roommate Kirk took me to an emergency room where I was treated for dehydration. I easily consumed two liters of intravenous fluid. Later, test results revealed that I was infected with "pathogenic e. coli."; which is roughly the same thing as Acapulco frozen *flautas*. The bill for the emergency room equalled what the entire three week trip had cost me, three hundred dollars.

TRIP TWO

January 15, 1993
to
April 25, 1993

V.
Returning South

The scent of brewing beer mixes with cigarette smoke in Carver's Brew Pub. Snow is piled deep outside and the roof beams above my friends Ken and Sarah, and I, are probably straining and as ready to snap as I am ready to dash southward to hot México and Central America. Sarah is pregnant and not drinking. They are good friends and they understand that, although I am eager to depart, the beer is really a sedative for the nervousness and apprehension that I feel. I always feel this way before major undertakings.

I pick up Sean McKelvie at seven the next morning. He'll be my traveling companion for a semester's independent study. I didn't expect my buddy Karl Geers to be ready and he wasn't. That's O.K.; what's a couple hours on a three-and-a-half month trip? Karl will shuttle my mighty Volkswagen Rabbit back from the border. The three of us finally connect up at Carver's, we down coffee, bagels, and donuts. Then we gracefully slide, skid, and splash our way on bald tires out of Colorado's snow and slush and into the deserts of New Mexico. We travel southward and downward in altitude to Paso del Norté, or, El Paso.

A year before I had made this very crossing. At that time I was scared. The man that dropped me off was also scared for me and reminded me, "Don't forget to say your prayers *down there.*" I said that I would. I think Sean was now saying prayers. Karl and I were experienced travelers in México, and Karl had also been to Guatemala, so while camping the previous night in a New Mexico state park, we, naturally, told Sean every Latin American travel horror story in the book.

The next morning, unfortunately, all of Karl's and my stories were substantiated when Sean was ripped off in the train station. Karl had crossed into México with Sean and I to check out Ciudad Juarez. Once we found out that the next train south was at six in the morning, I set off with Karl to look for the bus station and walk Karl back to the border. Sean stayed with our luggage. Some odd vapors, reminiscent of tequila, wafted from a building. We investigated. We ordered food and drinks and watched dancing girls doing the u46 (&^$#*R. Then I remembered whose car Karl was going to drive for the next ten hours and thought we'd better leave. At the border Karl swaggered across the bridge. I staggered back to find a dejected looking Sean.

Sean had been talking to a wiry little man who spoke English well enough to converse on any subject. They talked about religion and morality. When Sean turned his head the man thrust his hand into Sean's pocket and pulled out about 140,000 pesos (about $45. U.S.). The man ran like hell. With all the luggage to watch, Sean could only watch him escape. Now Sean was disillusioned with México and considered going back to his sweet fiancé. I encouraged him to give México another chance. Since my efforts to find the bus station had failed, we would have to wait for the train after all. It was only fourteen hours 'til departure.

We are now in Irapuato and nearing the completion of a mammoth thirty-seven hour train ride. In this heartland of México one leaves behind the hinterlands and the atmosphere becomes cosmopolitan, for the world's largest city is just a few mountain ranges away. The sombreros are replaced with modern hair styles, and live mariachi music gives way to a compact C.D. player playing Eric Clapton's "Tears in Heaven."

It's very hot, but I think of the snowy alternative back on campus in Durango, and I'm glad to be here. This train trip has gone much better than the last time I went this way. Sean and I had some good conversations, and when we were not talking I slept well. This time the train was cleaner, less crowded, and faster; although a bus would have been much quicker, it cost more. Now that I am here again, I don't know how I survived last year's trip. At least now I can understand most of what I read. On the 19th at 1:30 A.M., Sean and I arrived in Ciudad de México and walked to my old stand-by, the "Hotel Central Garage." We rented a nice third floor room with big windows.

We spent the next day wandering around via the metro. We went to the Zócalo, the main square, to find a *casa de cambio*. We walked through the wide space between the country's most important government buildings. Many of these buildings display an endless series of columns and arches. On the ground level are expensive shops carrying jewelry, Parisian fashion and every other expensive luxury. At the north end of the square the national cathedral looms over all, but to its right, though squat, sits the conspicuous ruins of *Templo Mayor*. This was the site of the double Aztec pyramids where the hearts of living captured warriors were cut out with obsidian knives and sacrificed to the sun.

Finally we were able to reach the people we were to stay with for a few days. Our plan called for us to stay with different people, then Sean would travel by bus directly to Antigua, Guatemala. I would head to the coast of Oaxaca to revisit Mezunte and Zipolite, per an assignment -the writing of a sociological report on the two villages for a professor back in Durango. Then, I would take the Pacific coast road in the state of Chiapas to Guatemala. From there I would make my way to the city of Antigua, and reunite with Sean.

The year before in Mezunte I had met Victor, and his brother Edgar came and picked me up at the train station. Edgar is very outgoing, and as he's into geology and the outdoors, I really have a lot in common with him. When we got to his house I finally saw Victor. It was a poor time for Victor to have a guest as he had lots of early morning work to do at the school.

On the twentieth I went by bus to Teotihuacán. The three big pyramids, and the extent of the ruins area is awesome. At one time it was an extensive city. I climbed the Pyramid of the Sun and The Pyramid of the Moon. Of the civilization that built the site of Teotihuacán, we know little. The site was a mystery even to Aztecs, some five hundred years ago. I left this site, one of the great mysteries of the world, in total wonder.

In the evening, Victor and I took a walk in his neighborhood and passed his church, the Mormon Temple of México. The rest of his family is Catholic, though Victor's religious preference causes "No problem whatsoever." Then we took a bus to the catholic Basilica de Guadalupe. The beautiful original architecture is falling down, a victim of earthquakes and uneven subsidence. In the new basilica we viewed, from a moving walkway, the original painting of the "Virgin de Guadalupe." It is a beautiful painting of the Indian Virgin casting her eyes upon the moving spectators with a caption that says something to the effect, "Don't worry; your mother is here... Your mother will take care of you." Everyone had expressions of love and devotion; tears rolled down the faces of many. Several woman were in rural-country traditional clothing, as the faithful had pilgrimaged from all over México. There was certainly a feeling of faith in the church.

Outside, Victor and I ascended the steps leading to the top of the hill, where in 1531, an Indian Virgin appeared to Juan Diego, a poor Indian, and the sighting's actuality was confirmed by Franciscan friars. This incident created a bridge between the Indians and the Catholic Church, thus helping the Indians to identify with Catholicism, while making it easier for Christianity to supplant previous religions. Before leaving the city I caught a subway to Parque (Park) Chapultepec and the Museo de Antropología. These subways are clean, modern and fast. La Raza stop has a long walkway with sophisticated photographs of other planets, the Earth, and other solar systems and galaxies. School aged kids were taking notes. To get U.S. students to do that, I thought, would be difficult.

Chapultepec Park is ornate with statues, fountains, buildings, gardens, walkways, and a dirty gray/green pond. Getting away from the noise and commotion of the city was nice, but I did not leave it all behind. Air pollution drifts in and leaves a gritty texture on each leaf. Many trees appeared unhealthy, as they had few leaves and many broken and dead branches. They might have been weakened by air pollution. As for me, my throat was sore and my eyes burned. This pollution is terrible, but it is evidence of México's rapid industrialization. Despite this, it was relaxing to sit at a patio café and sip orange juice prepared before my eyes in a press.

The museum is fantastic. The lower level is dedicated to archeology, and the top to ethnology. The museum is divided into displays of the various regions of

México. In a country as topographically and climatically diverse as México, many ways of sustaining life have developed. Here, too, students were taking notes and sketching. These students were of junior-high and high-school age.

In Oaxaca I saw a lot more than during my last visit. I discovered a *mercado* that covered many acres. When I first went through it it was night and I was the only non-Indian. There I tried some delicious, thin, tough beef cooked on wood coals. In the United States people like thick, tender, juicy steak. Latin Americans like their's just the opposite, and I am with them in this.

Going over the mountains was more difficult this time. On January 23, I took a 10:00 P.M. bus out of Ciudad Oaxaca in the hope that we would cross the Sierra Madre del Sur on a different and longer road than I had traveled the last time, thus putting me in Puerto Escondido around sunrise. I did not want to be dropped off in the dark, and I could sleep while traveling. From Puerto Escondido I would take a micro bus, or hitchhike, to my destination of Mezunte Beach.

As it happened, though, I ran into one of the information problems in México which are peculiar to people that are not fluent in Spanish. The route was the same as the year before, only this bus did not stop much and took each of the millions of turns as fast as if the road were a straight-away. I felt as though I was on a poorly assembled carnival ride, and though I could not see the roadside drop-offs for the darkness, worse, I knew that they were there. I couldn't help it; I leaned over and gargled into the driver's ear "*¡Enfermo! ¡Alto!*" (Sick! Stop!). The driver put self interest before company time.

In the early morning hours we passed Pochutla. I now realized that we would be passing near Mezunte way before dawn, and therefore I did not have to go all the way to Puerto Escondido. We were now on the coastal plain and barreling down the straight road. I asked the driver if he knew of the village of San Antonio. The driver slowly twisted his head around to face me and said that he did. He explained that it had no hotel, only a few houses, and that it was 3:00 A.M. He was truly concerned for my safety. I replied, *"Bueno."* He turned to face the road again.

He dropped me off as if I were going on a one-way mission. No people stirred in the pitch blackness, but the dogs gave me a riotous welcome. But it was nothing a few rocks couldn't handle. I walked down the dirt road toward Mezunte, five kilometers away. A little past the San Antonio Welcoming Committee, I thought of other things that might happen in the dark, namely that other dogs might not be so manageable, or maybe a carload of drunks might pass by and become curious about the lone *gringo* walking the lonely road. With these fears I found a nice strip of dust just off the road, unrolled my sleeping bag and went to sleep.

In the morning I noticed that the road had been widened since the year before, but not paved, as Oaxaca's governor had promised. The road used to be of a single lane, and grass covered in most areas. Now it is certainly "improved." Its two lanes are covered with one to three inches of dust that spits up with each step. The first and only car that went by gave me a thick duststorm to gag on. Though I had my thumb out, the new mini van with only one passenger and Virginia plates sped past.

Following the winding road, I was cheered by the sound of the ocean's surf beyond the fields and forest to my right. A few people were up and starting their day's work. The friendly Zapotec Indians greeted me with kind smiles and wished me, *"Buenos dias."* Mounting the top of the last ridge before Mezunte I could finally see the beautiful Pacific Ocean. I glided down to the beach and to familiar faces. Isabel says that my Spanish has improved. I shake hands with Javier and their three sons.

For the sociology paper dealing with the affects of tourism that I would write for professor Jim Fitzgerald, on a section of Oaxaca's coast, I made an effort to observe of tourists what the people that live on the coast see. Like the locals, I felt that a force from elsewhere was bringing changes that might not be for everyone's benefit. What follows, for the next several pages, until and including the paragraph that begins with the word "Overall", is some of what appeared in that paper.

Two slim twin sisters from Germany have the habit of running around nude on the beach every now and then. Although this was not unusual for Zipolite last year, a few kilometers down the coast, Mezunte is a modest place. The locals do not go nude, excepting the very young. The girls, in their early twenties, are with their German and English boyfriends. The group smokes pot all the time. A Mezunte teenager brings it to them. Strictly in the interest of academics, of course, I tried some too; one sometimes has to make sacrifices. This group lived out of a VW van parked on the edge of the beach. In the sand they had an open-fire kitchen. Diligently they did nothing all day, although the English guy was a good guitar player and practiced constantly.

Another group of foreigners was made up of three

Italian men, an Italian woman, and a voluptuous Spanish beauty. They rented Javier and Isabel's house, a five minute walk from the beach. It had a sweet-water well and they invited me to bathe. They were considerably more productive than the group on the beach, as they read and listened to classical music. To finance their stop-and-go, indefinite travels they made ceramic crafts that they sold to tourists. They laughed that people from the U.S., their best customers, thought that they were Mexicans, and that their bizarre crafts (distorted figures of witches, devils, and madmen) were associated with some kind of local ritualism. I give them credit for their imagination and humor, but they are spreading a steady chain of misconceptions.

There were individuals, too. Denny, a Frenchman in his early twenties, was a power-house of musical energy. Occasionally he broke the surf's tranquility with loud outbursts of Jimi Hendrix' lyrics, and the songs of other musicians. A couple of years before he had met the Spanish beauty in New Delhi. There she gave him the shorts he still wore. Off and on they seemed to be going together.

In the palm grove near the beach were scattered several vehicles with Canadian and United States plates. Besides these foreigners from other countries, there were a half dozen others from "The capital," Ciudad de México. They too were tourists in this "innocent provincial place," a rather naive and condescending label, I thought.

All foreigners had an obtrusive presence upon Mezunte's 350 residences. Several local men, in their teens and twenties particularly, seemed to hover around the foreigners and tried to socialize. A couple of them asked me for money. One guy, calling me his *"Amigo,"* asked me to buy him a shot of whisky. This never happened a year ago, no one begged or hovered about. Since tourism is new in this town, about two or three years old, perhaps there is a connection between some members of a subsistence culture, who see people on western style vacations, and begging.

All this idleness was not because of a lack of work in the area. Boats still went out to fish; Javier was building another *palapa* to add hammocks to his lodging empire -I helped him dig some post holes and put posts into them; a park was being hacked out of the jungle along a creek connecting the village square and a part of the beach; a new chain-link fence was being put up around the school's property; there was the old stand-by of clearing fields out of the forest for a few years' corn growing, until the soil was exhausted; but the biggest thing going was the construction of a "turtle museum." The construction of the museum was employing about thirty men; it was to replace the "turtle meat factory" that had closed four years before. Despite all this available hard work, foreigners were looked up to by the area's youth as an example of how to make it big in the world and go on vacation.

At any time Denny could change his musical style. One night he became a reggae artist with a more perfectly Jamaican voice than any Jamaican could sing. He was loud and clear and set an hypnotic mood which he was able to maintain all night. He was assisted by an impromptu band of a few acoustic guitar players, wood and leather bongoes, flutes, and tambourines and rattles that were swapped around. We had beer, wine, and locally grown marijuana. A fire on the beach provided all the needed light for our international ring of people. In this latter sense, tourism might be a good thing, but I doubted that anyone would be in working condition by morning, which was, of course, no problem for us tourists. I will never forget that night of fun, and I have never been so stoned, but on the down side I did not feel as though I was with real friends, and not, "It's like total connection. *¿No?,*" as the Spanish beauty put it.

A more tangible change near Mezunte is that the path out to spectacular Cabo Cometa is now easy to find as so many more people are stomping it down. I cannot imagine that local fishermen traffic could have increased that much. The wear on the path must be from tourists like me. The path, etched deep into the hill, is the tourists' mark upon Mezunte. From the high point on the cape one can see the sweeping crescent of Mezunte Beach. Other changes are more subtle and speculative.

Last year a beaten down wooden fence ringed Mezunte's school property. It is only a two room primary school. In January, 1993, a chain-link fence was three quarters completed around the property. It is as tall as a person. A sad thing about the new fence is that when the children were out for recess, they did not play. Instead, they clung to the fence where their mothers, grandmothers, and older sisters were on the other side. All stood together but divided, hoping that the bell would not ring. Before the new fence, the woman and some men would frolic around with the children every chance they could. I did not see those happy times, as I had only been there when school was out for Christmas. But Isabel told me that she did not like this fence, and how things had been before it. The youngest of her three sons went to this school. The older two went by bus to *"escuela secundaria"* (secondary school) a few kilometers away.

I wondered if the new fence had been put up to break down family relationships in order to better regiment the children into modern México. Perhaps then they could go all day without speaking a word of Zapotec, only Spanish. The establishment of a single language for México was one of the goals of the <u>Mexican Revolution</u> and its Constitution of 1917. Now 85% of Mexicans speak Spanish; the rest speak different Indian languages. In the state of Oaxaca, for example, there are said to be twenty languages. The goal has been being pursued for seventy-six years, and I suspect that México, although now more "unified" and "modern," is considerably poorer in cultural diversity, while the civil rights of many have been squashed. The opposing argument is that with the Spanish language the Indians can defend their rights. I think that argument is like finding a condemned man innocent -posthumously!

Aside from all the philosophical squabble, I think that the money could be better spent anyway. I have looked into the school through the windows. The benches and desks are rickety, there is one black board in one room. There are no maps, charts, or a globe in the school, and the shelves only have a few books. But at least the painting of Che is still on the outhouse door.

The turtle museum will be a source of income to replace the income lost from the ending of turtle hunting. I do not believe, however, that the completed project will be able to employ many people, since the star of the show, the *turtle,* an animal that people associate with slowness, is something that many tourists will go out of their way to see. Luckily, though, there is still no concrete hotel in Mezunte, again, as the governor promised last year. Although I had been expecting to see it under construction, unfortunately there is a good chance it will be built in the future.

Of the changes in Mezunte, I think the worst is the

example that foreigners are setting. The new concept of "eco-tourism" is trying to change the behavior of travelers. Basically, travelers should be a bit subdued and try to behave in a way that demonstrates respect for local cultures, as well as acquiring some self-education before entering new areas. Vacationers do not need to be saints -the Mexicans are certainly not- but they should try to have a little sensitivity. For instance, they should ask for permission before taking pictures. The success of eco-tourism, therefore, rests upon whether or not travelers will cooperate. This may be asking too much of some travelers, though, since it hints at being mentally challenging, and it might mean that the traveler would have to take an interest in someone other than himself.

Currently, of the people born in Mezunte and participating in the mixed employment/subsistence lifestyle, there is sense of dignity. However, in a full blown tourist economy, few of these people would have the urban skills needed to compete for the few good jobs that a tourist economy offers. They would only be eligible for poverty sustaining seasonal jobs, such as cleaning toilets or raking litter off sewage polluted beaches. For recreation they would seek the sort of cheap trills that some of Mezunte's young males are now. In the long run they would become bitter, like many of neighboring Zipolite's Zapotecs are; my next stop.

To avoid walking during the hottest part of the day I left Mezunte at first light for Shambhala, the "Buddhist ecological resort," at Zipolite Beach. The route took me through the village of Mezunte, past the old turtle factory, into tiny San Augustine, down San Augustine's long and nearly undeveloped beach, then up a hill into the woods to the back of Shambhala near the meditation center.

Emerging out of the woods, I walked the nicely swept

path lined with its kerosine jar lamps. I saw Carlos Luís sitting on the mound at the meditation center. It was fitting to see him first as I thought he was Shambhala's most interesting character. He had been gone from Shambhala almost as long as I. He had left with a new love to Michoacán, but left her after a few months and tried to catch a ship to the Orient. Although he had caught ships all over the world in the past, things were different now, and shipping jobs were hard to get. Lately he had returned to Shambhala and would begin running the restaurant in a few days. It looked like Jack Kerouac's On the Road and The Dharma Bums day's were ending everywhere. We had breakfast together. Gloria, Shambhala's founder, came to our table for a while.

Gloria had not changed a bit. She complained about the price of building material and labor to complete the rebuilding of the meditation center -burnt down "by the Christians"- and how it was hard to keep things going generally. As it was after the holidays, the place was uncrowded. I liked it better this way.

Despite her difficulties, Gloria had a small roof put over part of the meditation center and a new roof put over the restaurant. Her accomplishments were impressive. I think that it would be impossible for anyone to start anything like makeshift Shambhala in a place as developed and accessible as Zipolite is now. The world has changed. Gloria got into Zipolite before anyone else started in the lodging business there, which was eighteen years ago. Then it was only accessible by either a five kilometer walk, or by small boat from Puerto Angel. She is well enough established that she may just be able to keep Shambhala a going concern. Shambhala was built largely by volunteers, and they used mostly local materials free for the taking; people do not volunteer anymore, and, even here on this southern fringe of México, building codes are continually limiting what materials can be used in construction.

After breakfast I drifted down the beach past metroplex Zipolite. There were now a few cinder block buildings, including one three story structure. Someone had also attempted a three or four story bamboo frame structure. The top floor or two, however, crashed into the lower levels. Now it was abandoned, save for a new nylon tent on the sandy ground level. I would never camp in an unsturdy firetrap like that. I guess that all the new building codes were necessary after all, now that Zipolite Beach, at the end of a new and paved road from Puerto Angel, is accessible to anyone. No longer is it an isolated place where people must really use their heads when considering the capabilities of available resources.

Shambhala sits high on a slope and is protected from the sea by a massive rocky outcropping. Most of the old Zapotec village, right out of a Disney movie, is back from the beach behind a ridge. The bulk of the new tourist industry in Zipolite, though, is only one meter above the high tide and facing the wide ocean. With this in mind, I am confidant that the next hurricane will select which buildings, businesses, and people can stay and which ones can not.

Overall, in Mezunte and Zipolite, the tourist industry has had a negative impact upon the local population. For travelers it has mixed results. The development of the tourist industry here is too quick. Like cars colliding head-on on a superhighway, two cultures are meeting here with the expected gore. Better to bump and stall along grassy dirt lanes.

Leaving the beaches behind I took a short bus ride to

an intersection near Pochutla. I planned to take a bus or to hitch a ride along the coast to the Isthmus of Tehuantepec. Standing at the intersection was a Californian in his mid-twenties. He introduced himself and told me his life story, a major part of which was how he made a living scheming in Las Vegas. He was now headed for a resort down the coast, Huatulco, and would not settle for a ride from just anyone. "It's easy to get a ride here, but you gotta hold out for a rich Mexican; don't settle for some farmer's truck. There's lots of rich Mexicans. I mean, you get in good and you're set for dinner and everything." A mere micro bus came along. Having forgotten everything he had just said, he pushed me aside and got on and walked to the back of the bus. I sat up front. He had never even asked me my name; so much for eco-tourism, I thought.

On the way eastward the route passes by salt evaporation ponds, these are inside of large lagoons. The twisted, narrow, and hilly road goes in and out of valleys. The beaches, as viewed from higher parts of the road, are bordered by palm trees and surf and curved in long sensuous crescents, while back from the ocean huge sand dunes sweep up out of the narrow coastal plain.

But cresting one last high point in the road I had a view of what might be the ugliest town in the world, Salina Cruz. There were oil tankers and cranes, and the houses were speckled on sickly looking hillsides that were almost bare of vegetation. Garbage flew all about and the traffic was dense. I took a room in Juchitán.

In the morning I found out that it would be hours before the next bus, so I decided to try hitchhiking across the isthmus to Tapanatapec. I got a ride by asking directions at a Pemex station, one of the customers overheard me and offered a ride part way. This southern coast of the Isthmus of Tehuantepec, barely one hundred and sixty kilometers (one hundred miles) wide from the Gulf of México on the north to the Pacific Ocean on the south, is a low altitude, flat desert country. Here, one makes a big leap from central México to Chiapas, Yucatán, and the countries of Central America. This isthmus, together with Panama, barely holds the American continents together. Out of the rear view mirror I could see the eastern most part of the Sierra Madre del Sur, and looking forward, the Sierra Madre de Chiapas swept skyward. Crossing this land bridge eastward is to enter a land less rushed and less developed.

The driver was Julio and his brother's name was Manuel. In my honor they played a few tapes with music in English. I never realized how sad Simon and Garfunkel were until they asked me to translate a few of their songs. Later, when I explained to them that the gist of the song "Wipeout," by Venture, had to do with the impact of an accident, they were disillusioned. The next song, in counterpoint, was in Spanish and it implored everyone in the world to jump up and dance and sing. They dropped me off at an intersection where they were turning.

There, there were three guys changing a tire on a car that they were towing. This group was transporting a land cruiser and pulling a station wagon; they had a pickup truck loaded with bicycles, and a small, low clearance Toyota Tercell. They were going from Miami to Honduras. I rode with Armando in the Tercell. He is an Honduran doctor out having a little fun with his businessmen friends. The ride was over the rough, pothole ridden Pan American highway built in the 1940s. The caravan stopped to help a driver with a flat. He needed a ride to a town with the proper sized tire.

Here and there we stopped to search for one in the towns along the way. We traveled at least eighty kilometers to find the right tire in this remote region. From Tapanatepec to the Guatemalan border streams pour off the Sierra Madre de Chiapas and the country becomes greener and greener. This narrow coastal plain, one of México's most beautiful areas and least developed, is known as the Soconusco Coast.

At one town we stopped behind a long row of traffic. Armando immediately thought that there must have been some major auto accident ahead. However, laughing girls came to us to sell us tacos and tortillas out of straw baskets. They informed us that the bridge ahead was "broken" and would not be passible for "at least six hours." It seemed to me that a highway bridge would take much longer to fix. But the river, only a stone's throw in width, and stony bottomed, was only ankle deep with one short section about calf deep. Before you knew it, pickup trucks were charging down the highway embankment toward the river and plunging into it. Armando followed in our totally inadequate for the task Tercell. I got out in anticipation of pushing the car as I knew it would get stuck or stall. Water flew as the Tercell arrogantly sped across the river and I ran along behind it. I saw the muffler disappear beneath the waterline and the car bobbed as it floated downstream and hissed steam. But the car's momentum got it to the other side anyway and with a few spins of the tires on slippery rocks, the car climbed like a small wet duck out of the river onto dry land. I climbed back in and Armando shouted, "Did you see that? Everyone laughed as they saw me splash into the river!" I said, "I'm a little surprised you made it too." He replied, "I have faith in God!"

Under the bridge men were working with hydraulic

jacks to raise the bridge a little. I was not sure it would do any good. With today's huge trucks beating on the road built to handle 1940's sized vehicles, I thought the road needed a lot of general upgrading. I was surprised to see how much traffic was on the road. Armando said that the last time he had traveled this part of the Pan American Highway there were only a very few cars and light trucks. That had been 1980. He theorized that now that the Central American wars of the previous three decades were abating, people were returning home.

In the town on the other side we came to a gas station, a Pemex, to regroup our caravan and to gas up. Armando complained, "México used to have cheap gas; now it's expensive. I don't know why. You never know how big a liter will be in these places." To pay for the gas, Arthur, one of the businessman, traded a mountain bike.

VI.
Welcome to Guatemala

The border crossing at Talismán Bridge was the most confusing I had ever experienced. We arrived just after dark. Armando said, "The border closes at 8:00 P.M., but with Guatemala one never knows. Sometimes you can not pass if there's trouble with the guerrillas along the road." We passed Mexican customs with little difficulty. Men and boys were running all over the place incessantly bothering me to change dollars for pesos or quetzales.[14] Also, we were not yet over the bridge and into Guatemala when people were trying to sell souvenirs and memorabilia from Guatemala. Sure enough, this evening the border closed early; no reason was given. As I could not obtain a visa until 8:00 the next morning, and my friends, who already had their's, wanted to leave as soon as the border opened at 6:00 A.M., I took leave of them and found a hotel room. The three stayed out all night to take turns guarding their products in the pickup. My hotel room was a bare cell of concrete and an old bed, though it did have a shower, toilet, and sink, and it was only fifteen quetzales.

In the morning I got my visa, then found a bus to Malacatán. México is fairly modern, but Guatemala is said to be about forty years behind, and I would add that it is twice as full of surprises. In this rural part of Guatemala cars have not even come close to replacing horses. Cows and oxen pulling carts are common sights. Our colorfully painted old

---

[14]*One U.S. dollar bought about 5.1 quetzales.*

Blue Bird bus was packed to the max. There were eighteen double seats, seating for thirty-six school children; I counted seventy-six people of all sizes.

In Malacatán I changed bus for highland Quetzaltenango, Guatemala's second largest city. Along the way apathetic troops dragged their feet beside the road, and a soldier slept on the stone wall of a machine gun nest. At one point, before I could appreciate what was happening, the bus slowed to move through a crowd that was nervously looking down the road. They were watching three machine gun topped armored cars. The machine guns were pointed into the jungle. The bus driver accelerated to top speed and we swept behind the armored cars. I hoped that if whoever was in the jungle opened fire, that they would at least be good enough shots to hit the army vehicles and not our flimsy bus.

From the lowlands I could see the coastal chain of volcanoes that reach up to 4,220 meters (13,845 feet). On the mightiest volcano that I could see, probably Volcán Santa María, I thought I discerned a trace of snow. Parallel to the Pacific Ocean in Guatemala, the volcanoes are stately and symmetrical cones. North of this highest spine of the country are the Guatemalan Highlands, an area that ranges from 1,000 to 2,500 meters (3,500 to 8,000 feet) above sea level. Most Guatemalans live there, and so in a healthfully temperate climate. However, this year the country was experiencing its longest cold snap in history. Temperatures went as low as -7° celsius (20° F) and some indigent people had died. It is said that there is no heat in any of Guatemala's buildings, even in cold Quetzaltenango's hospital.

Eventually we climbed off the Pacific coastal lowlands and the road became very curvy, steep, and the air cooled until I was cold in my short sleeves. My pack was on top of the bus so I could not get to my jacket. Veterans of these lands had sweaters and blankets ready. Through a dense fog we crested a pass and descended into a valley with a huge landslide. Judging from the short and scarce plant growth on it, I doubted that the land could have slid but a year or two earlier. The debris on each side of the road was twice the height of the bus. The slide was two kilometers long and a quarter as wide. All the slopes in the area looked overgrazed and overfarmed, I thought humans were creating the conditions for more landslides. Dangerous as it was for the land's stability, the Indian farm plots, perched on the edges of cliffs as they were, made for an other-worldly scene. After another mountain pass we descended into the verdant and sheer walled Río Samalá gorge. The flat bottom was checkerboarded with garden plots while steep slopes of pasture swept upwards toward land that vaporized in clouds.

By Quetzaltenango I was very tired. I had traveled three days straight. I took a simple but adequate hotel room. In the city the streets are narrow, steep, and twisted to conform to the terrain. Luckily, there is nowhere near the ratio of cars to people as in the United States, or such a traffic jam would ensue that helicopters would be needed to pluck the cars out of the city.

Quetzaltenango is the site where, in 1524, Pedro de Alvarado lead an army of Spaniards and Indians (Tlaxcalans) from central México, perhaps totalling less than one thousand, engaged up to thirty thousand Quiché Maya, commanded by legendary Tecúm Uman, whom may or may not have actually existed, and beat them. But it was only the first and most spectacular of many battles that lasted well into the 1540s, and never really succeeded in conquering the Maya. This cycle of repeated small conquest differentiates the Maya from the Indians of central México. For in the entirety of the Maya landscape, which stretched form the Isthmus of Tehuantepec in México, eastward to the Río Lempa in El Salvador, and northward to include the Yucatán Peninsula, the Maya were an extremely fragmented people.

If a conqueror's conversion of a conquered people to its religion, language, culture, and society are measures of successful conquest, then the conquest of the Maya was only spotty and incomplete. Today the Maya are still to be seen in most of their original lands. It seems as though the Maya merely tolerate, circumvent, and make appearances for, rather than accept overlords. But this adaptation for cultural survival is beyond the scope of this book.

I headed out of Quetzaltenango by bus for a four and a half hour ride to Antigua. The entire trip cost twelve quetzales. I met Sean in the central park. He had arrived in Antigua the day before and was intent on staying there. For my part, I was shocked at all the non-Spanish speaking tourists, as there were so many of them. I considered leaving as I knew that the temptation to speak my own language would be great and defeat part of my purpose for being there; that of learning to speak Spanish. Subsequently, I was to discover that there were language schools in Quetzaltenango and Huehuetenango. I would recommend learning Spanish in those cities over Antigua, since you would be better insulated from hearing English.

In Antigua there are language schools everywhere. They are informal and provide one on one instruction (conversation might be a better word, writing and grammar are optional) with a native speaker, usually a high school student. You basically pay to have someone to have the patience to sit there, talk to you, and entice you to speak. All the schools seem to be set up about the same, a large room and courtyard with dozens of tables and chairs. Classes usually start on Monday, though they can accommodate anyone's schedule. School goes for four to six hours, which is actually pretty gruelling if you have a good teacher. It cost Sean and me $60. apiece per week.

The language school concept was brought to Antigua in the 1960s by the Peace Corps. Now they are no longer here since there are too many tourists, and too many students of Spanish that are only mildly interested in learning the language. During breaks in homework there's good night life to keep them entertained. There are so many schools here that it is obviously a lucrative business. Despite the poor language learning environment, Antigua is the "spiritual heart" of the nation, and must be experienced.

Antigua, at 1580 meters (5,200 feet) and in the tropics, has a climate that is often characterized as being "Perfect all the time." A walk with Sean up a hill on the north end of town revealed a beautiful view of the checkerboard blocks of the city. It is set in a basin surrounded by three great volcanoes to the south and southwest, and high ridges the rest of the way around. These volcanoes are Volcán de Agua (Volcano of Water); Volcán de Fuego (Volcano of Fire, and appropriately named, as it has erupted at least sixty times since 1524); and Volcán Acatenango, the tallest of the three at 3,976 meters (13,044 feet.)

Volcán Agua is so named either because its crater may once have supported a lake, or after the many springs at its base. As one story goes, the lake collapsed the crater wall during heavy rains in 1536. This flooded the second Spanish capital of Guatemala,[15] now known as Ciudad Vieja (Old City). The capital was then moved to where Antigua (Ancient) is now. At that time it was given the poetic name, and is sometimes still called, Ciudad de Santiago de los Caballeros de Guatemala (roughly, City of the gentlemen horsemen of Saint James of Guatemala). This capital, though, fell victim to an earthquake and an eruption and volcanic ash from Volcán Fuego in the year 1773, when the capital moved to its present location, Ciudad de Guatemala. The setting and climate are so idyllic, and the history of the place so interesting, that I decided that the tourists could be put up with after all.

One day Sean and I walked to Ciudad Vieja, then turned east to ascend through the farm lands on the slopes of Volcán Agua. Though the trail was in a littered gully, the volcanic soil on each side was rich looking. The many fields are of small size. Trees and shrubs dot them. Furrows were cut across the slope and whole corn stocks from the previous cropping filled the furrows for fertilization and erosion control. This considerable sized area was all hoed with human labor.

Halfway up the cone of the volcano we had a beautiful view of Volcáns Fuego and Acatenango, and the towns of Antigua, Ciudad Vieja, San Lorenzo El Cubo, San Antonio Aguas Calientes, San Andrés Ceballos, Santa Catarina Barahona, Santiago Zamora, San Miguel Dueñas, and Alotenango. Later I would explore most of these places. On our mountain the paths were becoming scarcer, though, and

---

[15]*The first was located at Iximché, about thirty-five kilometers northwest of Antigua. It was abandoned due to Cakchiquel Maya raids.*

along ravines groves of wild trees and vines stretched downward into the crop lands. We had to walk over the freshly hoed soil, but we were careful not to step on top of the rows where crops were planted. In many places beets, carrots and radishes were there for the taking, but we had too much respect for the hard work that went into their planting to steal any. The pitch steepened and we were faced with a wall of jungle.

We sought a path and found a good one. We followed it and guessed at the best branches to follow as it forked continually. Soon we were without any trail and just going straight up through thick brush. We broke vines and branches constantly. Ferns covered the slope to such an extent that we could not see the ground. Immense and slippery moss covered fallen trees had to be climbed over or crawled under. The edges of bamboo groves were fought through, but they made for easy going once inside. The sunlight passed into the lower level of forest with difficulty because of the dense forest canopy. Up higher the ground steepened even more, the forest thickened, and the leaves were wet from passing clouds. We were exhausted and Sean had only a little water left; I had consumed all of mine and most of his. We conceded defeat and turned to stumble down the mountain, but we vowed to try again.

A week later, on Saturday, February 7, Sean and I set out to tie the score with the Volcán de Agua. This time we were not so spontaneous and had looked at a map to discover that there is a jeep road on the opposite side of the mountain from where we had tried the week before; I took more water this time. On the dusty dirt road outside of Antigua on the way to the mountain's base, waiting for a bus, or a car to stop, four Toyota land rovers and some Jeep Cherokees sped by and left Sean, some Guatemalans, and I coughing in a cloud of dust. In the vehicles were pale faced, blond and brown haired people from the U.S. I muttered, "Damn rich minorities." We took a bus to Santa María de Jesús. In the town were numerous soldiers, some in sandbag enclosures. I knew from my language instructor that about a year prior there had been guerrilla activity in the area.

The hike was easy. First we passed through a wide belt of farm fields. Above that is a broad leaf, vine and fern entangled cloud forest. In this area a lot of firewood is cut. Men and boys carry the firewood down the mountain loaded on mules, or on their backs with the weight on a tump line across the forehead. Near the top the cloud forest gives way to a pine tree and grassy floored forest. But the road we were on was really chewed up.

Perhaps the road was needed to get the radio and T.V. towers up there, but why keep it open to the wheeled public that tore up the road and made a lot of unnecessary noise? Within a kilometer and a half of the top there was a place where the road was altogether washed away. At this terminus were the six vehicles that had ignored us earlier. From here the going could only be done on foot. We had huffed and puffed up to that point while others just ripped up the mountain. It was not that we wanted a ride to where they had been able to drive, but if everyone parked in Santa María de Jesús, the mountain would be much more like the nature preserve that it is officially designated. It was tempting to let the air out of all the tires. I did not; in Colorado I might have. Near the top we passed the people from the cars as they were heading down. By overhearing their conversations and seeing their "WordPerfect" caps, it was confirmed that they were from the U.S. This raised the dilemma of how I, as a foreigner, could complain about how Guatemalans took care of a mountain when it was people from my own country that were the ones chewing it up.

The summit area was dotted with many radio and television towers. Cables to balance the towers are stretched everywhere. But the air was nice and cool and reminded me of high altitude Colorado in the summer. It was cool enough for frost in the shade, but it was dry, sunny, and pleasant. However, due to clouds at or just below our level, much of the view was obscured. Once below the clouds on the way down we could see the capital, Ciudad de Guatemala, Lago de Amatitlán, and Volcán Pacaya, which was spewing smoke. On the walk down we avoided short-cutting the switchbacks and followed the easily descending road. In places it is like a tunnel of green through the trees.

Through Sean's and my conversations in English, with a few words of Spanish thrown in, our discussions helped us to articulate the ideas coming to us from the many impressions we received in México and Guatemala. For instance, in Ciudad Juarez I told Sean that I did not give to beggars. That was true, then. But in Antigua, for some unknown reason, I had given to some beggars. It seemed as though I had softened, but I knew that in Guatemala something was different. In this conversation I realized that the only beggars in Guatemala were people that were too old to work or severely handicapped. In México, as in the U.S., all kinds of people had begged from me. In Guatemala begging is a livelihood for those who would otherwise starve. I noticed that Guatemalans of no great wealth, ordinary working people, also gave to beggars. This was done in a way that was not showy at all, rather, with easy understanding. Coming to this realization might not have been possible unless I had someone to speak to in my own language. For this reason a traveling companion is good, even though it slows down the learning of another language.

At any rate, language class is going well this week, and I'm learning a few things, despite my health going up and down. These past two weeks, the first with Xavier, the next with Juan Carlos, have advanced my language skills. I now find that the less I think about what I'm saying in Spanish the easier it comes. I am picking up a sense of other things, too.

In Antigua, the Guatemalans seem to be putting themselves at an economic disadvantage by allowing foreigners to open businesses and buy property.[16] In Antigua it is becoming difficult for Guatemalans to compete with the foreign currencies, and individuals from the rich industrialized countries are creating a sort of expatriot society of leisure, with Guatemalans as their servants. This country should at least protect itself by allowing only Guatemalans to buy property. Antigua is so desirable in its romantic colonial ruins, architecture, and climate, which is true of much of the country, that foreigners often buy property and live here, part or all of the year. My language instructors agree that this is the situation, and they are resentful of it. Where I write from now, Doña Luisa's, is a café owned by a former Peace Corps volunteer. My favorite hangout is the "Café Liberia," or the "Rainbow." It is owned by an English woman and a man from the U.S. This seems to

---

[16]*This was true in the late nineteenth and early in this century, but then it applied to U.S. banana and German coffee planters who bought up large tracts of rural land in the east and northeast of the country. Today it is happening here in Antigua, the "spiritual heart" of the country.*

be the case in "tourist areas" and "vacation spots" in many of the nicest places in the world. I can not help but picture Antigua as a future Provincetown, Massachusetts, an "artists' colony and gay community," there are already many artists here, and some gay people as well. Or perhaps it will become another Vail, Colorado -expensive enough to keep the poor out. In either case any semblance of civic life erodes away to part-time, fair-weather residents.

While Sean and I were in language school we stayed with a host family. One night we had a talk with the father of the house, Antonio, and he told us his income and shared his thoughts about Guatemala with us. He makes only 348 quetzales per month, which is about $69 U.S. Antonio works for the city driving a dump truck. Life in this rented house is comfortable, although a bit noisy. Everyone pitches in to barely make ends meet. His son works in a bank and doubtless earns more, as do son and daughter in-laws, whose children are baby-sat by Carmen, Antonio's wife. Everyone comes here from work or school and eats the wonderful lunches that Carmen cooks. Sean and I each paid the family $30. per week.

Besides all the hardships of the economy, Antonio says that when people complain about low wages, the police silence them. The police stop certain people to check identification papers -which are never right because of constantly changing laws,- then they put you in jail and fail to notify your family. Once you are gone long enough your family comes looking for you and the whole situation becomes an expensive and lengthy problem to get out of. Sometimes they keep you in jail for days. This sort of harassment is how the government keeps people quiet.

What I have observed, then, is what people do in the

normal quest for a meaningful life. They turn inward to the warmth and security of the extended family, while keeping quiet so as not to lose ground in their material existence. Perhaps partly because of this form of oppression, Guatemala has families that are very close. Besides having fun together, they have a subtle understanding and compassion for one another, all knowing what an unfair society they live in. In the family sense, then, it is obvious that Guatemalan families are more "advanced," or "developed," than many in the western industrial countries. However, in this country at war with several guerilla groups, it is not hard to understand why people are not enthusiastic about supporting their government. I have often heard it argued that political reform would take care of the country's economic ills, as well as deflate the claims of the guerilla warriors.

People also turn to religion, especially the Catholic Church, and mixtures of pre-Columbian religions and Catholicism. In recent years certain Evangelical sects have increased in size. I shall not examine the voluminous and explosive subject of religion here, other writers have already tried this, and although I have plenty to add, I shall try to remain faithful to impartially reporting what I saw and experienced.

After two weeks in language school and living too close to too many people, and daily looking up to the beautiful volcanos of Acatenango and Fuego, I could not hold myself back any longer, it became imperative that I get out of town and enter the wilderness. So I loaded up with two gallons of water, bought four mangoes, some bread and cookies, and took a bus to Ciudad Vieja. From there I hitched two rides to La Soledad. Cresting the summit of a pass on the way to the village, a view of volcanoes and valleys explodes. La Soladad is just a small hilly crossroads in farm country. One got a wild west feeling, and no town has a finer panoramic view.

I ascended the well used trail between gardens to the broad-leaf hardwood forest and its jungle underbrush. At just the point that the grass and pine forest begins there is a flat area on the ridge, a good campsite. If anyone ever tells you that it does not rain during the dry season, such as the bartender at the Rainbow, don't believe him. Wet clouds swabbed everything and light rain was driven by strong winds. I didn't have a tent, so my first thought was to get a fire going. Then, with fishing line and a Swiss Army knife equipped with a saw, I built a lean-to. I used sticks, brush, pine needles and grass for material. On the fire, just outside my shelter, I brewed tea. I kept dry inside, although I knew that if it rained hard or for long it would become as soggy as being out in the rain. But shortly after dark the stars shone.

The morning was very windy. I started hiking before the sun found my part of the mountain, as I was on the northwest slope. I passed four Guatemalan boys on their way down from a higher camp, and two guys that spoke English immediately afterwards. They were the last people that I was to see for two days.

Even in the pine forest the wind was very strong, and a light coating of frost covered the ground. Breaking treeline the view opened unimpaired, except for the mountain in front of me. The north slope was grassy, but the broad top of a false summit, Pico Yepocapa, was a moonscape of black cinders. On the south slope of Yepocapa was a metal shelter. I stopped there to eat lunch. I continued down to the col where the funneled wind made me think seriously of returning to the shelter, but going up the final pitch was less windy. On this very steep part, however, the cinders rolled down under each footstep, making for difficult going. Here I was wearing wind pants over blue jeans, and a flannel shirt, fleece jacket, and a wind breaker with a hood. Boots and gloves covered the rest. At the summit the wind was enough to knock a person silly. At times it was all I could do to stand. The old crater is a city block in size, though not deep, just dish shaped and smooth. From the top I could see numerous other volcanoes to the east and west, and glimmering blue Lago de Atitlán to the northwest. To the south the Pacific Ocean was visible, through the haze. To the north, most of Guatemala was covered with clouds, and only highlands stood clear.

Descending required little effort as I glissaded the loose cinders to the woods below, southward, toward a pass called La Horqueta. In this way I lost several hundred meters, and I would certainly have hated to have been going up that loose slope. Southward was my next day's goal, Volcán Fuego. After a hike part or all the way to its summit I would return to La Horqueta, then walk eastward for an easy descent of the mountains toward the town of Alotenango and civilization. The pass was all grass and pine trees and sun. There was already a good lean-to set up, but I decided to use it only if it rained.

Although there was a path from Acatenango's summit down to this pass, I did not see a path that led downward from the pass. This problem perplexed me and I spent a considerable amount of time scouting for such a path. Although a descent through these upper mountain environs of pine trees would be easy, the difficult part would be in the densely vegetated cloud forest zone, and there the grade would steepen, too. I knew that I might end up on top of cliffs, for which I did not have repelling gear, and that routes along streambeds might be blocked by dry waterfalls. Other than going back over the summit of Acatenango, though, I really didn't have a choice. My supplies at this point consisted of three quarts of water, some bread and two mangoes. I had plenty of tea though; so why worry about tomorrow? As I lounged reading a book, something stirred in the tall grass just a little way off. It was a small deer, nowhere near the size of a New England whitetail, or a Colorado mule deer, but a deer, a rare sight in Central America. As I reached for my camera it became aware of me and bolted into the forest. From the sound of it there were at least two other deer running with it in the forest.

   I got up in the early morning, took a camera and one quart of water, and started up Fuego's slight path. I had intended to go only as far as what looked safe, for I had never before ascended a mountain spewing smoke. I came to a steep ridge with slopes falling away for a thousand meters on each side. The volcano was not throwing rocks or cinders; only a steady stream of smoke and steam. Before long, cautiously stopping and deciding not to go any further, but taking just a few more steps anyway, I found myself at the sulfury smelling smoky summit.

   Usually I take pictures of the view from a mountain. Here, though, the summit area and its crater absorbed all my attention -and film. Rather than feel afraid I began to feel quite comfortable. In fact, as the air was cold, I used a steaming heat vent to warm my hands. There is a danger in being overtaken by the sulfurous gases. Luckily, though, a steady wind was blowing from the east. By staying upwind of the vents I was safe, even when as near to this Devil's breath as I was.

Back at the pass, feeling proud of my accomplishments, and imagining the great stories I would tell back at the Rainbow. I gathered up my pack and headed for my next destination. The going was good. A dry drainage provided an easy cinder path with some steep slopes to glissade. I hoped that the route would be this way the whole way down.

Soon, though, I came to the first dry pourover. This certainly slowed my forward momentum. I had to negotiate a detour over loose ground, through brush, then lower myself down several ledges by grasping trees and vines. This was hardly a taste of things to come, though, as the drainage developed into a full fledged canyon with a series of pourovers.

The brush thickened below each pourover. Each of these dry waterfalls increased in height. The detours became harder and more dangerous, as well as more difficult to find. Finally, I decided to get out of the canyon. I fought my way up through downward pointing brush. This was like charging bayonets. Ground slipped out from under each step and cinders kept filling my low cut boots. At the top of the slope I came to a wall of rock. I tried a couple short climbing routes but the rock was crumbly. Finally I found a good place to climb by clearing away plants, dead leaves, and dirt. With a burst of adrenaline I hoisted myself up the cliff.

Above the canyon the going consisted of bushwhacking through brush and vines that I needed to untangle, break, and pull down or lift up in order to pass. The vines often got caught between my neck and the top of the backpack. I could see the advantage of a machete, if I had only had one, and why Julian Duguid called the jungle a "green hell." However, I acknowledge that it was my own lack of preparation and inexperience in this environment that was making things difficult. Worst of all, I was now out of water and my mouth felt like dry cotton, and my tongue was becoming swollen.

Although I was walking on the canyon's rim, dry ravines plunged toward the main canyon and nudged me in that direction. This made it necessary for me to continually cross these formidable ravines. I had to be careful to cross at the right place, or I would be funneled to a point overlooking both canyon and ravine. Although I could not see the land's contours for the vegetation, geologists would refer to the volcano's steep slope drainage system as "consequential," that is, directed straight down and determined by gradient -in this case complicated by a canyon between two volcanos. The course that I had to maintain, therefore, was to traverse sharply to the right while still loosing elevation. As hard as going down was, going up the mountain to the pleasant alpine world of La Horqueta was clearly out of the question. If I had had plenty of water, though, I might have considered it, then labor up the steep cinders of Acatenango and down the trail that I had ascended from La Soledad.

Descending into one consequential ravine, though, it was clear that the vegetation was not going to let me climb out. Downward in the stream course was the only way to go. In this way I at least had gravity on my side to help me plow through the brush. The vegetation made the ground impossible to see. I am not sure how Tarzan did it, but swinging from tree to tree on vines is harder than Hollywood makes it out to be. Instead, I tried to stay on top of fallen trees whenever possible. However, at one point my limb ran out into a sea of green plants. I tossed my pack before me about two meters. It lay springing on a mattress of vines. I took a deep breath and leapt to it in sitting position and legs straight out. Upon landing the trampoline broke and I crashed two meters or so to the dirt streambed. The pack stood resting on my head and was held in balance by the vines.

Assessing the situation, I noticed that it was relatively clear, if a bit cramped, under the vines. For the most part the streambed was free of obstacles, mostly just brittle dead branches. Rushing water in another season had cleared the way. The advantage of not re-emerging from the plants occurred to me, and it struck me that I could kick my pack downhill in front of me to break the sticks and clear a tunnel-way beneath the vegetation. This worked for a few minutes, until I saw the opportunity to crawl out of the creek to higher ground on the left. Now I was on a peninsula surrounded by air. I was between the impassible ravine and the canyon. Luckily, though, it looked possible to descend into the canyon, and I sensed that I was getting to the mountain's base where it would fan out and become less steep, making the canyon passible. With gingerly moves and by shimmering down tree trunks I came to the bottom of the main canyon. It was getting dark and my eyes were playing tricks on me. I thought that I saw water stains on a cliff; a spring at last! But upon closer inspection, after crossing a boulder field, I realized that it was only a dark, sinuous tree growing against a gray cliff. My thirst increased.

By then the gradient was leveling out, and the next pourover was hardly thirty meters. From this dead end was a pleasant view of Alotenango, only four kilometers away, but I knew that I would not get there that night. Ascending a slope to get around the obstacle, I came to a couple strands of barbed wire. Out at last! I thought this was the edge of a farmer's field. Furthermore, there was a slight path and some food wrapper litter that I was glad to see, for it meant human life and their works that make life easier. There was a fire ring and some stacked wood -then nothing. The trail soon evaporated. Back to the dense forest and vines. I was no where near any farmer's field. Had I come upon a former encampment of soldiers, guerrillas, robbers? Campers maybe? Then why the barbed wire? The possibilities were exciting, but I did not feel like exploring for booby traps. However, in exchange for a few glasses of water, I would not have minded meeting with even those that I had hoped to avoid. Rest stops kept getting longer and longer. At one point I cut open the now empty one gallon water bottles to lick out the drops of water in them. This worked to wet my tongue a little. During these stops I noticed more and more wildlife. Birds of many varieties and number inhabit these woods. It darkened more.

Rounding the day's last pourover I stumbled onto a wood cutter's path and set myself down against a macheted tree stump. Here I am, I thought, back in civilization and I can't move. I did not have strength enough to pull out my sleeping bag for a good half hour. An owl landed on a branch a dozen steps in front of me. It stared at me. I stared back. Contemplating how near death I felt, and might have actually been, I rested waiting for it to call my name[17], but it did not. Moisture came back to my mouth, the owl flew off, and I knew that in the morning I would enter town.

---

[17]*Being that I felt as I did, I recalled Margaret Craven's novel, <u>I Heard the Owl Call My Name</u>; had I, my time remaining in this life would have been short.*

In the morning the path certainly made things easier, although it occasionally disappeared and I would be left bushwhacking until I picked up the trail again. Still there were steep slopes to ascend and descend, and even at the mountain's bottom there was no water in the creek bed. Within ten minutes I was as thirsty as I had been the day before. I was there toward the beginning of the dry season, so most of the green vegetation that had made the going so tough was still on the brush and vines, yet there was no water to drink.

Climbing one last very steep slope that had been the ridge of a lava flow, the first field on the mountain burst into view. It was a partly tilled corn field. I was still in the cool morning shadow of Volcán Agua, which was to the east across the valley that Alotenango sits in. I climbed down a cliff for the last time and sank to my ankles into the soft rich dirt of the field. I was still a half hour's walk from town, but I knew a path would lead from this field to others and get wider all the time. Half way to town I met a small boy heading uphill with a machete. He had a small, old bleach bottle containing water, which he automatically handed to me. I took only a small sip as I knew he was going to be doing hard work in the forest and would need his water. A while later I met a man walking his horse uphill. On the horse he had a few large gallon containers of water, and from his supply I drank heartily.

VII.
Adrift in Central America

Although I had intended to travel directly to Nicaragua by bus through Honduras, a safe proposition I thought, while avoiding dangerous and impoverished El Salvador, I accidentally landed in El Salvador anyway, and there began a short, but most emotionally straining, time of my life. I say "emotionally straining," and not "emotionally moving," because while I was there I tried to block out of my mind what I was seeing. But the images kept forcing themselves on me. After a few days in a better place, Matagalpa, Nicaragua, it all caught up to me and the words flooded my journal, moistened by a few tears.

My Latin American history professor, Michael Fry, now in Durango, had done his doctoral research in the little town of Mataquescuintla, located in the Eastern Highlands of Guatemala. He had suggested that I might like to visit the town, and that I would see how its "Latino" society contrasted with Guatemala's Indian society of the Western Highlands, where I, like most visitors, spent most of my time. Mataquescuintla, by way of a small detour, was on the way to the Honduran border and my intended trip to Nicaragua, so I decided to go there. After a couple of days rest from my adventure on Volcáns Acatenango and Fuego, I set out from Antigua on the crowded buses.

I had anxieties about the necessary bus transfer in the capital, Ciudad de Guatemala, because large cities are not my forte, and my Spanish was still poor. The funny thing is that every Guatemalan that I asked directions of had a hearing problem. In this way, if you amputate "Mataqu" from "escuintla," you end up traveling south to the Pacific coastal lowlands and the city of Escuintla, instead of eastward to a highland area near the Honduran border.

I checked into a hotel, then I wandered around in the sweltering heat of the town for a couple of hours and wondered how my good professor had lived in this humid environment for six months. I attributed this to his being from Louisiana. That night while looking at a map on the hotel's patio, the establishment's owner, who spoke English well, came to chat. After a while he figured out that I was not where I thought I was. With great effort he politely held back his laughter. He kindly set me straight. I felt like a helpless and hopeless idiot. At any rate, correcting this mistake would have meant going back to the dreaded capital and all of its hearing problems. Nicaragua seemed so close if I were to just hurry across El Salvador, jump on a boat and cross the Gulf of Fonseca. Yes, it was a plan I could live with, despite the fact the I knew the whole route would be in hot and humid lowlands. Mataquescuintla would have to wait.

In the morning I had breakfast with the hotel owner and his wife. Afterwards, he took me to the Salvadoran consulate to get a visa, which would not be possible at the border. The chubby consul pulled up to the small concrete building in a brand new Ford Bronco. He wore a suit while the other two passengers were in security uniforms. I asked the consul if it was safe to travel in El Salvador. He said that it was safe, and he added that everything was fine: The war had ended two months ago, there were lots of tourists, good food, good beaches, good nightclubs...

On a bus on the poor roads of the Guatemalan coastal plain it took hours to get to the border. We passed through sugarcane plantation country where Highland Indians descended in the hundreds of thousands for several months every year to work under deplorable conditions.[18] There were no tourists here, save for me. The pothole ridden road was really something to complain about, the driver flew along and the turbulence almost dislocated bones. The bus driver, in my honor, popped in a Johnny Cash cassette. But Cash was out of place here as he would hardly be able to earn a few *tortillas* per day in a place like this.

With no fanfair I left Guatemala. Little traffic passed through this border with the high sounding name of Ciudad de Pedro Alvarado, and the place felt tranquil. A Salvadoran guard was sleeping while leaning against a tree. He held an M16 with a finger on the trigger. I hoped that a fly wouldn't bite his neck. He never even knew I walked passed. Customs was difficult though, as the officer went through everything I had in excruciating detail. I think that for a moment he feared that my water filter was a dynamite detonator. After a while he decided that I was harmless and wished me a safe trip.

I jumped on the only bus leaving the border, which was heading to San Salvador, the nation's capital. The road was among the nastiest I had ever traveled. You could tell that the road had been a wide and paved avenue at one time, but now it appeared to have been literally bombarded. It was full of heaves and depressions and the bus had to dodge from

---

[18]*For a description of this mass migration, see I, Rigoberta Menchu: An Indian Woman In Guatemala, by 1992 Noble Peace Price winner Rigoberta Menchu, ed. by anthropologist Elisabeth Borgos-Debray, trans. by Ann Wright.*

side to side following two ruts to avoid piles of upended pavement, rubble, and ruined truck parts. Along the road's sides all the trees had been burnt, beyond them were lush green sugarcane fields that stretched toward the muggy distance. Concrete bordered irrigation canals flowed with water. The few shacks along the way were the most dilapidated I had ever seen. The countryside was relatively depopulated, but what people there were all found the bus.

The bus became packed beyond capacity. A gritty dust billowed up from the holes in the floor. In Guatemala I left behind a mostly dark-haired race of people; here the population was mostly of European heritage. The Salvadorans' clothing was not colorful and their hair was brown or even blond. They also seemed thinner and hungrier than the Guatemalans. No one smiled.

Not quite halfway to the capital, and just before dark, I had had enough. In Sonsonate I decided to find a hotel. A rush of people throbbed forward desperately trying to get on the bus as I tried to get off of it. On the side of the road hundreds of people had set up tiny businesses to sell all sorts of things from clothing to food; oddly, small bottles of shampoo were the most common manufactured item. Everyone's clothing was soiled and ripped. The people here were skeletons. There were many people with amputated limbs, some even had bloodied casts. I had never before seen such poverty, and I am sure, as I rewrite this a half year later, that many of the people I saw in Sonsonate are now dead. I ignored the people that approached me to sell things or asked for money. I knew that what I could give them would not make a dent in this town.

Everyone's eyes were bulging as though an army of ghosts had just stormed through; this town was a ghost. A traffic light dangled by a few wires; buses and sugarcane trucks barreled through the intersection at will. Potholes in the street and on the walkways were a foot deep. There were many broken windows and doors. Everything seemed in need of demolition and reconstruction. There was human waste on the streets. Mysteriously, though, there were some people and businesses that seemed completely unaffected.

Wanting to get out of the crowd I entered the first hotel that I found. It was the Hotel Florida. They had the nerve to charge twenty colons[19] for this place. I got a filthy little room on a littered courtyard. There I met an Italian that perplexed me because he seemed to be perfectly at ease in this place. His name is Arturo. He was making his second trip around the world. Now he was on the sixth month of a nine month travel stint. This time, he joked, he was traveling from west to east so as to get to Italy an hour earlier. He was traveling with a good pack and an expensive camera, and, as I was to find out, on a remarkably small budget. I was hungry, so I asked him to join me for dinner. He was not hungry, but he agreed to accompany me and to show me to a modern restaurant that served good pizza and coffee. He was right, it was very good, and he thought so too as he ate half my pie. I wanted to introduce him to my brother Ron in New Hampshire, who had sometimes called me a "freeloader." But I am only cheap; Arturo is a freeloader!

Nonetheless, Arturo's conversation was worth a few dinners across El Salvador, for his several observations of other countries and how they compared with Latin America, particularly Vietnam, were very insightful. Of Vietnam, he said that it was poorer than Sonsonate, but there were other

---

[19] One dollar bought about 5.5 colons.

differences too: He never felt threatened by the Vietnamese - they do not come up to strangers and put a hand on your shoulder or grasp your elbow; Latin Americans always have to be touching someone, and they can be pushy, especially in marketplaces. Poverty in Vietnam is consistent, and everyone has equally little; Latin American poverty is patchy, with rich and poor communities and neighborhoods adjacent to one another. The Vietnamese are of a mostly uniform race and culture; Latin America is incredibly diverse. In Vietnam you can count on not finding medicine or modern amenities; in Latin America, in many places, you can have anything you want, you can even live in absolute luxury -if you have money. In Vietnam there were many Australians, some Canadians, and Europeans, but no U.S. citizens; in Latin America there are many U.S citizens in big resorts, though surely not in places like Sonsonate. Here there are more travelers from overseas than from the U.S., though it is attached by land.

  I was not feeling well so I decided to stay another night. If the Hotel Florida were Sonsonate's only lodging, I would have forced myself out of there, but luckily I found a decent hotel. It was four stories high. The rooms were arranged in the shape of a horseshoe, all their windows and doors opened to the inner court. The end without rooms was walled off for the entire four stories, and the entrance in the wall was through metal doors and gates for cars. From outside it looked like a totally non-functional block of concrete. The inside had a café and gardens and safe parking for the several expensive and new cars. On the roof was an Evangelical chapel. The ugliness of the street below was far enough away so that the eye wandered over roofs and tree tops and the distant countryside. This place was only five colons more. It was too much for Arturo, so he stayed where he was. I could rest here, but I knew what was outside.

Now Arturo invited himself to travel with me to Nicaragua, which was still fine with me. We took a bus to San Salvador. On the way we passed endless sugarcane fields. There were no houses in the countryside. All the people lived in crowded towns and villages between the seas of sugarcane. There didn't seem to be enough houses for all the people, and they looked like they lived outside. People were obviously poorly fed in all these unsanitary places, yet little of the country's rich volcanic soil is used for growing food crops.

Most of these lands are owned by El Salvador's infamous "Fourteen Families." They use the country to grow cash crops for export. They have built elaborate irrigation works to water their sugar fields, banana crops, and such. They are also involved in growing coffee beans, cotton, and raising cattle. All of this is for export. In college I had read books about this unfair land distribution system, and I knew that it was one of the main issues that had fueled twelve years of war in the country, but I never thought that the inequities would be as plain to see as the view from the roadside to the horizon.

It is fashionable in the United States, especially among those that call themselves environmentalists, to blame all the problems of the Third World on over population. But now, I began to speculate what this country's people would look like if the land were planted with food crops for domestic consumption. In 1992 it was estimated that there were five and a half million people in the tiny country, thus giving it around 269 people per square kilometer (679 per square mile.) The population density of the U.S., for comparison sake, is only twenty-eight people per square kilometer (seventy per square mile.) I suppose that if El Salvador's land were divided up among the poor, and they grew their own food, this land might be able to support double its population. Although there may be an overpopulation problem here, to suggest that the problem of malnutrition in the country is attributable only to "There's too many of them," as I've often heard, is racist and naive. A high population density does not automatically lead to poverty. It does lead to problems, but these can be overcome; certainly any reasonable landless Salvadoran peasant would see it that way -thus the war.[20]

We didn't see too much of San Salvador. What stands out in my mind was a tall glass-mirror covered building with half its windows busted or gone. The bottom floors were boarded up. 1989 had seen the war's most vicious and widespread fighting, and it swept through this city too. I imagined a guy with a machine gun spraying the glass-mirror building and enjoying the sight of raining glass.

The Farabundo Marti National Liberation Front (F.M.L.N), a coalition of groups that are as diverse in ideology as Socialism is to Catholicism, waged a fight against the U.S. backed central government and military, whom they say are arms of the Fourteen Families mentioned above. They controlled a good 40% of the country, mostly the area near the Honduran border. Victory for the F.M.L.N. seemed just around the corner.

Now, however, the country is in what I believe to be no more than a calm between storms. Two months prior, the

---

[20] *Germany has 216 people per square kilometer (559 per square mile), while Japan has an incredible 328 people per square kilometer (848 per square mile). Both countries have a higher per capita income than the U.S.*

outgoing Bush administration in Washington had mediated a cease-fire between the government and the F.M.L.N. All through the war years the F.M.L.N. had stated that anytime and under any conditions they would come to the bargaining table. With the end of U.S. military aid imminent (five billion dollars in loans), the central government decided to call the F.M.L.N. on their offer. This call put the F.M.L.N.'s credibility at stake. They came. The little country came out well: The U.S. canceled four billion dollars worth of loans; the F.M.L.N. forces were to be incorporated into the national military and make up one third of its total size; free and fair elections are scheduled to be held in 1994.

However, although the cease-fire is working for now, there are problems. The general national disarmament is going badly; people seem to be hiding weapons. Also, there is the problem of *"delincuencia"* (delinquency or crime), there are a lot of armed men in the country that have sophisticated weapons from all parts of the world, left over from the war, and they are practiced in the use of these. With the war over and not enough employment, whole patrols of now unemployed and armed men walk into banks and other businesses and take what they want. No ordinary law enforcement organization could control them. It would take a huge army, but now there is not enough money to support such an army.

Elsewhere there was a lot of rubble, too, but the unmistakable sign of new pavement indicated that the economy was picking up. Salvadorans have a reputation in Central America as being very industrious, and for this reason it was predicted that the country would recover from its dozen years of war "in no time at all." There were also new businesses. These were involved in electronics, auto parts, car and truck dealerships, and various stores. New buildings were being constructed. There was a sense of hustle and bustle. Unlike the countryside where there were no cars, many people here drove cars, and with that impatient Latin attitude that only comes out behind the wheel. Here, things were obviously richer; no wonder everyone in Sonsonate was so impatient to get here. Throughout Latin America, the state of rural abject poverty is fueling the growth of a few cities, usually the capital of the nation.

We changed buses for La Unión, on the Gulf of Fonseca, from where we hoped to take a boat to Nicaragua. On the way we passed over moderately high lands and more agricultural country. The bus descended into the Río Lempa valley and less populated country. In the past motor vehicles could cross the river on a high modern bridge, but our bus made a sharp right before the bridge and meandered down to the river bank. There we crossed the river on a makeshift bridge.

With some spans missing, the tall ruins of the former bridge loomed up above. It had been blown up in the war by the F.M.L.N. This was meant to cut the country in half, and it effectively did this. La Unión, in the country's extreme east, was cut off from the capital, but it never fell to the rebels. From the bridge I could see upstream to the massive concrete dam holding back Embalse 15 de Septiembre (Reservoir of the 15th of September), which was also attacked by the F.M.L.N., probably as a symbol of irrigation for the Fourteen Families' agribusinesses, to hurt the economy, and make a big splash in the news.

The only city of any size was San Miguel. Like the capital, it too had many new businesses and was graced with new pavement. This had been a rebel stronghold, and with the cease-fire, I understand that there were some horrendous retaliatory actions here that almost undid the cease-fire as soon as it had started. According to a Californian now living in La Unión, government troops killed five or six thousand rebels; their corpses are now buried under the city's streets. Back hoes dug trenches, then bulldozers pushed the bodies into the ditches and covered them. Then the beautiful paving job was added.

Credible documented truths are hard to find, it's almost like the stuff of a madman's imagination. But even if what I heard was only half true, the atrocities were horrendous. Something that made a big news splash, while I was in Central America, was the Salvadoran president's pardoning of all war criminals and human rights abusers. The United Nations' Truth Commission had just published a report attributing 95% of all the war's atrocities to the government and its agents. It seems that the government did not want too many rumors to be investigated.

We crested one last hill and the Gulf of Fonseca came into view. I had expected a malarial lowland swamp and estuary, but instead it was a massive expanse of water with a rocky shore and surrounded by hills and volcanoes. The bus dropped us off at the dirty main square and park of La Unión. "¡La Unión Soviética!" was jokingly announced.

We immediately walked down to the piers and got all sorts of answers about transportation by boat to Nicaragua. Certainly there was no auto ferry. I had been counting on a ferry. A newsletter from the U.S. embassy in Ciudad de Guatemala advised traveling U.S. citizens not to go to eastern El Salvador, as it was too "dangerous." They advised, "If you must go to Nicaragua at all, go overland through Honduras." They were vague about what was dangerous, and why one should take the longer highway route to Nicaragua, rather than going in a straight line from Guatemala's capital to Managua, Nicaragua, that country's capital, via the ferry. The discovery that there was no ferry was annoying, but I shrugged it off as there seemed to be an alternative.

There were large motorized dugout canoes. These could make the forty kilometer crossing, with a stop at an island, in three and a half hours. These canoes are anywhere from five to ten meters long, and as much as two meters wide. The people that skillfully hacked these out of huge tree trunks left a thin wall all the way around. Nevertheless, they all had bail buckets for water that came in from cracks in the wood. There were a dozen of these boats in a jetty embayment. Some sort of navy security shack stood nearby.

It was about three o'clock, and according to teenaged Marine guard Carlos Molina, who spoke a few words of English, there "might or might not be another boat today," and "tomorrow, maybe." He held an old rifle that looked as though it was ready to fall apart. Figuring out the customs procedure was a problem, too. Where were the customs people? Who were they? Did they really care if we checked with them before leaving the country? Did we need to pay a little money to an official, maybe? These were hard people to find. They lived, "Up there in town." After some discussion with Carlos, and a couple of hours, Arturo and I gave up and went to find hotel rooms. I was running out of cash and had the bright idea of waiting to cash a traveler's check until arriving in Managua the next day. But things were not to go that quickly.

We found a decent hotel five blocks away. We wandered to the town center but couldn't find anything appetizing to eat. Several people asked me for money and I gave change to the first three beggars. After that, on my low budget, I really couldn't give any more. Arturo hadn't given anything. We met a guy standing in the doorway of a drugstore. He was in his twenties and from a family in La Unión which owned several businesses, including the drugstore. He spoke English well as he had just returned from five years of study in Toronto. I asked if he had liked Canada, as it is a country that I love. He said that Canada was O.K., but he liked El Salvador better, because if he needed anything done, such as his laundry, house cleaning, yard work, or just a woman, "People here will do anything for even a little money." He warned us to be careful in the town's main square, because all the poor people were really desperate for money to eat, and, like himself, we looked very rich. It's true that just about everyone in the square gave us the creeps by staring at us, and at times I wondered if homeless men, bag ladies, and street kids and babies alike would spontaneously rumble and kill us, but I'm one to be open-minded and trusting.[21] For this sort of possibility he showed us a hand-gun under his suit coat. He recommended a restaurant to us in a "better part of town." He promised to join us there when he closed the drugstore, but he never did. Maybe he was killed on the way.

  The restaurant was laid out as a series of different level decks connected by steps and bridges. All this was on stilts and over the water. The waitresses were beautiful and wore very thin dresses. Their figures stood out. El Salvador is often said to have the world's most beautiful women, and

---

[21]*For the record, I have always held this attitude while traveling, and I have never carried a weapon. This has never failed me.*

here they were. The smell of the ocean was in the breeze. We ordered fish dinners. All the patrons were casually but well dressed, and no one looked like they had missed any meals lately.

    A band came to our table and played a loud raspy tune. They would not leave until I tipped them. It had been a long day in just the sort of muggy climate that makes me irritable. It was now nine o'clock and cooling off enough so that I was just unwinding. The second bottle of beer was doing its trick. As I was finishing my meal, I felt a tugging at my leg. It was obviously a dog, and it was annoying the hell out of me. I kicked my leg around under the table trying to get rid of it. Then I kicked more furiously. I had had enough bothers that day; I hadn't come into a nice restaurant to be bothered. Finally I looked under the table. The meek, dark, and thin face of a little boy looked up at me.

    He could have only gotten there by climbing around under the decks, on rafters that patrons never saw. Perhaps he waited for food scraps to accidentally fall off tables and into the water. Arturo then looked under the table, smiled at the kid, and threw him his fish bones and head. The kid scurried back under the deck like a rat. Then there was a pull on my shoulder. A slightly older boy stood beside me and asked for my plate. I looked to Arturo and then all around, waiting for someone to tell me how to respond. There was a loud cursing from the kitchen and a fat man jumped down some steps toward our table. Arturo quickly handed the boy his plate. The boy turned and sprinted away toward the gate he had come in as the hollering fat man chased the kid, but he couldn't catch him because he was now limping as if he had just sprained an ankle.

    Clearly the restaurant would not have beggars. Arturo

and I went back to our conversation about European football as if nothing had happened, and that was fine, although I was a little unnerved. I tried to forget about it with another bottle of beer. When all was settled down the older boy came back with the plate licked clean. He put it on the table and gave a clear and charismatic, *"Gracias mis hermanos"* (Thank you my brothers) so that all the restaurant could hear. No one paid attention. They carried on with their polite conversations.

The next morning I was sick and wasn't going to take any boat anywhere, even if there was a yacht ready to go and the customs people rolled out the red carpet for me. I had experienced this sickness in Antigua a couple of weeks before while staying at Antonio's house. Since I was familiar with all its symptoms, that of being weak, hurting all around, and having an especially upset stomach, I was not worried; I knew it would pass in about twelve hours with one final hurray. If I could live through the last part I knew that I would be fine. That night the sickness passed on schedule, and so we began making plans to hit the harbor hard the next morning, demand service, and get to Nicaragua.

It was the same old port, but now little bits of information were falling in place. The next day "they" would come to our hotel an hour before a boat was to leave. All that we had to do was show up. This gave us another day to wander around La Unión Soviética and see all the sights. Beside the harbor there was a Navy and Marine base. It was behind a solid concrete wall perhaps ten meters tall, complete with a crenelated top. It also sported towers every fifty meters or so. Soldiers stood guard. It could have been a Medieval castle except that it was painted in a camouflage green and brown pattern. This wasn't to hide the fort. Nothing could do that. It could have only been painted that way for psychological effect, or to give soldiers something to do when their regular trade was slow.

The Californian mentioned earlier was a retired man from a U.S. aircraft company. With the U.S. cutting back on arms manufacturing he was let go on a small pension. He had been in La Unión for two years because he felt that his pension would not support him in the United States. He dealt used cars on the side. I spoke with him for quite a while, but somehow I got the impression that he was more than he let on. He said that La Unión had been the most lawless town in Central America until about 1990. The war had cut off La Unión from the capital, and it was under military rule. Everyday in the main square there were four or five executions. In the hills behind town, F.M.L.N. guerrillas and government soldiers played out bloody combat. Sometimes there was shooting up and down the streets and around the fort. La Unión had to be held; there was no way out for the soldiers who were there, and if they were captured they would have been killed. Before the war La Unión had handled almost half of El Salvador's exports. Its good harbor was coveted by the F.M.L.N., as it was the only obstacle to an easy sea route to the aid that Nicaragua might be able to provide. The attackers were frantic, the defenders were desperate, and the stakes were high.

At eight the next morning, a customs agent came to our hotel and had us woken up. We got to the harbor as quickly as possible and were ready to go. Hours went by. I took a short walk out on the jetty, and there in the hull of a boat, just below me, were the sleeping boys who had come to us in the restaurant. So this was their home, I thought. If by chance they do not die soon in their dangerous world, they're going to grow up to be two tough and fearless guys. The look on that little boy's face under the table came back to haunt me, and I shall never forget it. Now when any subject of social inequity or war comes up, his is the face that I see.

Arturo was irritating me as all he could do was complain about the price of the boat ride, about thirty colons. However, it was pointed out by my California friend that going to Nicaragua by land was more expensive, it took three days, and it was "dangerous." I spoke to Carlos Molina to while away the time. I asked if many foreigners came through here and took a boat to Nicaragua. He answered "Oh yes." How many every month? "Four of five." He hadn't traveled much, but he had heard much of the United States. He was shocked that I had never been to Los Angeles, and that I had no desire to live there or to even visit. He desperately wanted to go to L.A. I told him to get a better gun.

A pickup truck came by with two unshaven and rough looking good-ol'-boy types. Without getting out of the truck, the passenger called us over. He showed me some I.D. in his wallet and said to hop in back. Helpless, I looked to Carlos. He gave me a nod to let me know that it was O.K. We were whisked off to the customs office in town. There our passports where stamped. To formalize the situation I was offered a shot of whiskey. Back at the port we were set to leave as soon as an agent wrote in the date and collected some small amount of cash -I had the satisfaction of knowing that this irritated Arturo. We waded into the water to a waiting dugout canoe.

About twenty people got on, and all sizes of boxes and shapes of nets were haphazardly loaded. We had life jackets for about half the passengers. The jackets were so poor that I doubt that any of them would have floated. Ladies used them to keep the sun off their heads. I was the only one to bother wearing one. The safety strap broke as I tried to tie it. On the way someone was always bailing as water kept springing up from several cracks in the floor. Two guys had to restrain Arturo as he was excitedly jumping around taking pictures. He didn't realize that he was nearly causing the boat to flip.

  The island we stopped at is called Meanguera. It looks like a self contained world of steep hills and valleys. There are many tall trees and garden plots, and some cows and goats wandered around. There are houses near the sea at the outlet of each valley. At the island's little beach port there were fish drying in the sun on racks. There was no modernity here, no electrical wires and no sugar plantations. All but seven of us got off. This was the last I was to see of Salvadoran soil. According to my California friend, it was untouched by the country's twelve years of bitter war, and so perhaps it could be called a time capsule of what once was on the mainland; a better place, a better time, peaceful and independent.

VIII.
Nicaragua

Whereas between La Unión and Meanguera we were in a sheltered part of the Gulf of Fonseca, now the boat was in the wide mouth of the gulf and we roller-coastered over big waves and got splashed each time the bow came off a crest and hit a trough. I waited for the boat to splinter to pieces but it miraculously held together. We aimed at 857 meter (2,812 foot) Volcán Cosigüina in Nicaragua, which is shaped like a lean-to and sweeps dramatically out of the sea. All is placid now, but for a few days in 1835, this mountain acquired its present asymmetrical shape from what had been a symmetrical cone, in one of history's great volcanic eruptions. The blast and earth movements were so great that islands and shoals rose from the sea, rivers on land changed direction, hundreds of kilometers of sky were blackened with ash that floated groundward to kill vegetation, and locals thought that this was *"La Ruina"* (The Ruin, or, the end of the world). The reverberations were not just local; those in Kingston, Jamaica, heard it *eight hundred miles away!*, and people in Europe read about it.[22] But this would not to be the last time that an event in Nicaragua would send its reverberations around the world, and in many ways it was not the loudest or the most earth shaking.

In the 1980s the Reagan administration did all it could to destabilize Nicaragua; this is not doubted or denied by any-

---

[22]*See John L. Stephens' excellent* Incidents of Travel in Central America, Chiapas and Yucatan, *vol. 2, (Dover Publications, Inc., New York) pp 36-38.*

one. However, I shall not delve too deeply into politics, as others have done this.[23] Instead, I shall describe what I saw and experienced, and, perhaps, better knowledge of this feisty country will help us to better understand our own society and its dependence upon technology and money. Like Vietnam, Nicaragua, a small Third World country, shook the mightiest country in the world.

We beached near the old auto ferry dock, while the ferry itself was half submerged and rusting in the water. Potosí's customs office is in an old corrugated tin warehouse. Myself, being from the U.S., only had to pay two dollars for a passport stamp. Arturo was irked because he, as an Italian, had to pay $20.

Nicaragua is five times larger than El Salvador, yet it only has three and a half million people. This gives Nicaragua a decidedly rural and even frontier character. Along the rough dirt road between Potosí and Chinandega there are numerous small farms. In their fenced fields they grow corn and other crops. People live in tropical looking grass and wood houses. There is livestock everywhere. Unlike El Salvador, where one sees very few animals -they were eaten a long time ago,- and only sickly ones at that, Nicaragua is a land of fast horses, fat cows, and dangerous bulls.

We passed ponds where kids were swimming and

---

[23]*See Walter LaFeber's* Inevitable Revolutions: the United States in Central America. *(W.W. Norton & Company, 1984); E. Bradford Burn's* At War In Nicaragua: The Reagan Doctrine and the Politics of Nostalgia. *(Harper & Row, 1987); Bill Weinberg's* War on the Land: Ecology and Politics in Central America. *(Zed Books Ltd., London and New Jersey, 1991); Michael Dodson and Laura Nuzzi O'Shaughnessy's* Nicaragua's Other Revolution: Religious Faith and Political Struggle. *(U. of North Carolina Press, Chapel Hill, 1990); and, especially, Leslie Cockburn's* Out of Control. *(Atlantic Monthly Press, 1988), for more information.*

swinging on ropes over the water. Horses galloped with robust people on them. Oxen pulled large two wheeled wooden *carretas* with tall loads. I didn't take this ruralness as poverty, I looked at it as self-sufficiency. Here, unlike El Salvador, it is possible to be self-sufficient for two reasons. The first is that there is more land and less people, with the accompanying natural and free resources of the land, such as wood, thatch for roofing, and soil and water for sustaining life. The other is that since the 1979 Sandinista Revolution, and the disposal of dictator Anastasio Somoza Debayle, who personally owned half the country's arable land (which he devoted to cash crops for export), people who had been landless peasants now have access to land. These people do not have to huddle together in filthy roadside encampments and work seasonally for the big land owners; here they can be independent.

We arrived in Chinandega at sunset. There was confusion about a bus to León, a destination that we were obliged to provide to customs, so we decided to stay here. Arturo complained about the prices of hotels so much that a taxi driver told us he could take us to a place where we could stay free. He dropped us off at the *Cruz Roja*, the Red Cross. I was embarrassed, but Arturo was pretty pleased with himself. They allowed us to sleep in the conference room and there was no limit to how long we could stay.

The people in the small city were openly friendly. In the town square there was a basketball game and it looked like the whole town was out to enjoy the evening. There were no soldiers. Along with one of the guys from the Red Cross, we took a tour of the town in an old fire truck. There were some strange looking carriages here. Some of them had been cars or vans at one time; now they were totally stripped down to make them lighter for the horses that now pulled them. This sort of horse drawn carriage would be considered an aesthetic nightmare in the U.S. Here, though, in a land that had experienced a war economy for so long, it was completely practical.

In the morning I said so long to Arturo. I had been trying to get away from him for a while. Although we agreed on many political and philosophical matters, he was unpleasant with anyone we met who showed any sign of wealth. He was convinced that all these people were crooks, which I am sure is true of some of them, but I at least give everyone a chance. On the other hand he certainly felt for and was always sympathetic toward the very poor. For this I must speak well of him. He liked Chinandega so much that he's probably still there, and has altogether forgotten about Italy.

When he walked me to the bus station I couldn't help getting in a jab. Arturo liked taking pictures of people who were "pure, uncorrupted by money and greed." He always asked before taking pictures and got people to give an honest, if not a confused, smile. Once when he took a picture of some kids, said *"Gracias,"* then turned to take some more pictures, I went up to the kids and told them to go collect their *propina* (tip). I like those Chinandega kids, they learn quick, Arturo was soon surrounded by five of them demanding money.

For no particular reason I headed to Managua, the capital. I had accomplished my goal of getting to Nicaragua, and now all I had to do was absorb what I saw and try to talk to people and get a feel for the country. However, even these simple tasks were made difficult because I still hadn't regained my strength from the sickness I contracted in La Unión. In León there is a university, I thought that there I might find some stimulating intellectual discussions about the country's politics, but I didn't feel like talking that deeply. Then I considered going to Granada on Lago de Nicaragua, a huge and historically significant lake. Before the route through Panama was chosen for a canal, this lake was on the most seriously considered route; it is still discussed as an alternative canal route.

The bus passed by the huge water body of Lago de Managua where volcanic cones spiral upward. Although all was beautiful, the heat was sapping my strength. I had to get to a cooler place. I considered traveling all the way through Nicaragua to the cool highlands of Costa Rica, but that would be a lot of traveling and defeat my purpose of getting to know Nicaragua a little. So, from the sweltering capital, I took a bus north to the country's highlands, such as they are, to Matagalpa.

Malagalpa is about 760 meters (2,400 feet) above sea level, and although it's no where near as high and cool as the parts of Guatemala that I like, its climate was an improvement. It is a small city and I felt safe walking the streets at night. It has a certain historical and current affairs significance as well. This northern region, near the Honduran border, is where many of the Contra raids of the 1980s took place. In the town of Jinotega, just fifteen kilometers north, there was some sort of trouble going on with the "Recontras." They had gathered together a group of eighty or so heavily armed men and occupied the town to get national attention and make statements and demands. They claimed to represent five thousand fighters, and demanded that certain people in the government resign, namely Sandinistas in high positions, such as Defense Minister Humberto Ortega, the brother of former Sandinista president

Daniel Ortega. In addition, another group of Recontras had set up a road block on the main highway through the north, Highway One, which would be my route out of the country in a couple of days.

But Matagalpa has a cultural life of its own, too. I was there on Ash Wednesday, and a procession of perhaps a thousand, led by a priest, sang it's way through the city's streets. That night the streets were deserted as everyone was in the cathedral.

One peculiarity about Matagalpa is all the brand new Toyota Land Rovers. It is rugged country around here and these are the right cars for it. I was told that many people in Matagalpa had gone to the U.S. during the war years. In the U.S. (I wondered if some had only gone to Honduras to become Contras) they were able to earn a lot of money and bought Japanese vehicles. Some of the houses were very well kept and looked expensive. This town is nothing like Chinandega; it's wealthier, and harder to talk to people, too.

I took the bus to the lowlands and Highway One. There I waited and waited for a bus going north. Asking guys standing by the road when a bus might be by, they shrugged and said *"No sé"* (I don't know). A large freight truck with several men in the back came to a stop and a couple of people beside the road ran and heaved their packages into the back, and they called for me to do the same.

The truck was going all the way to Ocotal, near the Honduran border. There was a father and his young son, several young guys, and a large black man who spoke English with a Caribbean accent. He was originally from Bluefields, but had lived in Ocotal for the last twenty years, and was that community's sole minority. He said that all his friends were there and he never experienced discrimination.

His profession was that of a lumberjack, but work in Nicaragua in recent years was slow, and he has been all the way to northwestern México to find work. I asked if he thought things might get better in Nicaragua, he replied, "No, they are getting worse."

I also spoke to Edgard, a former member of the Sandanista army. I asked if he liked the Sandanistas, but he shook his head and answered negatively. He had only been released from the army because he had been shot in the stomach by a Contra; lifting his shirt he showed me the wound. Now he worked for the man whom owned the truck we were in. His job was to help with the loading and unloading, as well as to ride in back and keep an eye on the sacks and crates of products. The passengers essentially paid for the gas of this tri-weekly run between Ocatal and Managua. Passengers would occasionally knock on the roof of the truck and it would come to a stop. The passenger would then confer with the driver and hand him a couple of *cordobas*. Other passengers were picked up periodically. I had, evidently, found the northbound Highway One bus.

We came to the broad highland valley where the city of Estelí is located, and where the Recontras had blocked the road two days before. Now all was peaceful. Only the black man, Edgard, and I were left in the truck. We stopped at the driver's relatives' very modest house for a cup of coffee. There were many children and adults in the three room cinder block house. Though the furniture was sparse the matron sat me down in a comfortable chair and the coffee never stopped flowing. Later, upon arrival in Ocotal, I offered the driver some *cordobas,* but he refused to take them.

One of the amazing things about the Contra War in the 1980s is that the Contras were never, despite copious quantities of U.S. arms and money, able to occupy and hold a single Nicaraguan town. They just raided now and then, then they would retreat over the Honduran border where the Sandanista army would usually not chase them. A June 1, 1984 raid on Ocotal is representative of a Contra raid. Six hundred to one thousand Contras swept into the sleeping town in the pre-dawn; they indiscriminately unloaded rounds in all directions, burnt down the sawmill that employed two hundred and fifty people, burnt the electrical plant, and severely damaged a coffee-processing plant and storage bins. Then they left. Almost one hundred people were killed or wounded. The people of Ocotal were left to cleanup, bury the dead, and try to rebuild in a country that couldn't get loans from its traditional source -the United States.

Ocotal is a pleasant town of only about a thousand people. On the whitewashed walls of the town are paintings of Augusto César Sandino, Daniel Ortega, and Che Guevara, and none of these are defaced.

IX.
Two Wars, Economy, and Timing

In the park in Ocotal I had some quiet time to reflect upon the previous several days of travel. There I sorted out my opinions on two matters, and how they relate to two wars. The first regards the functioning of the economy of a small country, and the other, far more complex, involves the timing of the more-or-less successful, and thus far unsuccessful revolutions in Nicaragua and El Salvador, respectively. It is often said in the U.S. that the Sandanista government, which came to power in 1979, was a failure because the country's economy steadily declined after about 1982. This is not strictly so, though, as when one considers what the little country was up against, it is amazing that the Sandanista government survived at all into the late 1980s.

All Central American countries lack an "economy of scale," that is, of a large scale. Thus, it is like any state in the United States if cast off from the rest of the country; albeit though Central American countries are more accurately comparable to Alabama or Mississippi, than to, say, New York or Illinois, this only strengthens my point. As such, the tiny countries need to draw upon the resources of a larger entity to run their daily business and to conduct long term development. Although only a matter of speculation, if Alabama were to be economically blockaded from the rest of the U.S., the result might be economic collapse for that state. This sort of blockade happened to Nicaragua. Some aid came to Nicaragua from Europe, but this was a time when Europeans were starting to look eastward through increasingly large holes in the Iron Curtain. But Nicaragua persisted, admittedly with many mistakes such as the forced relocation of Miskito Indians (to distance them from the Honduran frontier and Contra influences), to carry on.

Increasingly, though, resources both financial and human had to be pulled from development projects to deal with the immediate problem of deflecting Contra incursions away from communities and economic infrastructure, and chasing them out of the country. It can be calculated that the twenty-thousand-man Contra force north of Nicaragua in Honduras, is the hypothetical equivalent of the U.S. having a hostile army of one million three hundred thousand located in Canada, and making periodic incursions deep into our country. Bearing this in mind, an economic blockade and constant harassment, the Sandanistas held up pretty well.

Since <u>World War I</u> every war has suffered more civilian casualties than soldiers. Today, war is not just young men shooting at each other, one side trying to kill the other side's soldiers. This is only the ideal form that a war might take. Rather, what war is all about is making the opponent's society suffer as much as possible. To demoralize a population it is necessary to undermine the legitimate authority of the opponent. This is done by eroding the opponent's economy through the destruction of their infrastructural base. Targets become dams and bridges, water lines, gas and oil lines, the harming of harbors and airports, electrical lines, and all communication equipment, and the destruction of forests, livestock, and crops.

Added to this are propaganda and fear tactics to draw a population's heart from the government, or to make them fear helping a government that they may like or are indifferent to. Related to this is the killing of community leaders, such as members of the clergy, teachers, aid workers, and government representatives. There is also the propaganda of letting the world know that trouble exists, while scaring off tourist dollars, and making the country seem a risky place for outsiders to invest money. The idea is to make the enemy's population hurt profoundly.

In El Salvador, as victory for them was so near at hand, the people sustained a loss when the reformist F.M.L.N. settled for peace. In Nicaragua the opposite is true, and now the people are better off for it. Although El Salvador held the posture of a democracy in the 1970s, it is evident that voting was hopelessly corrupt, and only small concessions to land reform were being made. There, the infamous "Fourteen Families" held most of the arable land, and, like in Samoza's Nicaragua, used it to grow cash crops for export. The Fourteen Families also control the military, which would have been completely untenable against the F.M.L.N. if not for five billion dollars in U.S. "aid." The Fourteen Families reportedly live in Miami, and their influence in the U.S. is certainly greater than that of the F.M.L.N.'s.

All through the war years of the 1980s and up to late 1992, the F.M.L.N. had consistently said, sensing their limitations vis-a-vis the U.S. backed military, that they would go to the bargaining table any time and under any conditions to make peace. At the end of the Republican White House, and necessary U.S. cutbacks in "foreign aid," because of the U.S.' own enormous financial difficulties, the Fourteen Families saw that their arms and money pipeline would imminently dry up, so they called the F.M.L.N. on their offer to settle for a peaceful solution to the country's problems. This left the F.M.L.N.'s credibility on the line; yet so close to victory. I, personally, would have forgiven the F.M.L.N. no matter what they did to obtain victory, but, in a country like El Salvador, where honor at the national level is so scarce, it is a precious thing.

Today El Salvador stands in limbo. Elections are scheduled in 1994, but leaders in the F.M.L.N. say that they will resume the war if they do not win. This may seem coercive, and it is, but against the backdrop of the country's history it is perfectly understandable. The Fourteen Families only appeal to themselves, the military that protects their interest, and a few managers. The vast mass of starving people that I saw are kept around only as a pool of cheap labor. The Fourteen Families control such things as vote counting and have never been honest.

Nicaragua had an immense advantage over El Salvador in the area of timing. 1979 was a time when the U.S., during the Carter Administration, was a country that was concerned with such things as human rights abuses, so the Somoza regime did not settle well with Carter, whom, though he was not pro-Sandinista, certainly did nothing to support Somoza. By contrast, the Reagan/Bush White House enthusiastically supported the Fourteen Families in El Salvador.

In addition, at the time of the Sandinista victory the Soviet Union was still vigorous enough, by way of Cuba, to support the Sandinistas. The F.M.L.N., on the other hand, who were at least partially encouraged by the success of the Nicaraguans, escalated their fighting too slowly and a little too late. Meanwhile the Washington scene was changing. So, whereas the Sandinistas consolidated their hold on Nicaragua in time to meet the gathering strength of the Contras in exile, the F.M.L.M. in El Salvador ran into an already established military with seemingly endless U.S. financial and weapons support.

In conclusion, the Sandinistas pulled off a successful revolution. In 1990 the Sandinistas peacefully gave up the presidency in democratic elections. By doing so they strengthened their claim to favoring democracy. Now they are in a position to come back to power by legal, non-violent means, and it would be impossible for the U.S. to object to their return without being condemned by the rest of the world as being imperialistic.

In contrast, the situation in El Salvador has degenerated to the point that most people are so destitute, depoliticized, and scared, that renewed fighting would be nothing short of a chaotic and desperate slave revolt. This is, however, not the fault of the F.M.L.N., they couldn't have known, anymore than anyone else did (or could prove to and convince the U.S. public), that the Reagan/Bush White House would commit itself so fully to the Fourteen Families, or that Soviet Block support would fade so quickly.

X.
Honduras

The border stations faced each other at the crest of a gentle ridge. On the Nicaraguan side the buildings consisted of bent up, rusted, and bullet ridden sheets of corrugated tin leaning against crude frame works. During the Contra War their buildings had all been destroyed. Across a space of a hundred meters, whitewashed buildings with shade porches made up the Honduran border station. This contrast was to last throughout Honduras, since, though it is reportedly this hemisphere's second poorest country, Haiti being number one, it has avoided the all-out wars of the 1960s, 70s, 80s, and so far of the 90s, that its three neighbors have suffered. This is not to say that all is wonderful in the country, though. In the 1980s the country was heavily militarized as part of Reagan's plan to contain the Nicaraguan "threat." Although Honduras had been fairly democratic and blood free until the 1980s, now it is poised for internal warfare that it had previously not been capable of, and in the next few days I was to see examples of this.

The small bus made its way down from the cool ridge to a blazing valley where I was to change buses for the capital, Tegucigalpa. I really just wanted to blaze through the country and go back to the comforts of Antigua, as I didn't think Honduras would be very interesting, and I wanted to get back to Antigua for *Semana Santa* (Holy Week), for which the city's celebration is famous. So here I was in a crowded bus station where nothing seemed to move, even the flies didn't move, and it would be "about" four hours before the next bus. I couldn't stand it, I had to get out of there. In Central

America it is possible to "travel" all day and only make a hundred kilometers, sometimes less. This can be God-awful frustrating, so I went and woke up a taxi driver. I talked him down from his asking price of 120 lempiras[24] to eighty for a lift to the capital.

In his rattletrap taxi we peeled out of the dirt parking lot throwing up a cloud of dust in the windless air. The dust must have added to the gloom we were leaving behind, but without me at least the flies could rest. The highway was good and there were only occasional stretches of potholes. We drove up incredibly long hills to pine forested crests, then down into wide valleys that were invariably hot, dry, and treeless. Men in the distance wandered about on horses. And again, the buildings that I could see were all admirably constructed and kept.

At one point we stopped at a granitic cliff from which cool fresh water poured. The driver assured me that it was the best water in Central America. We drank from it heartily. He topped off the radiator and we went speeding off and only suffered one flat tire before he whisked me into the capital.

He dropped me off at a very expensive hotel. Passing two heavily armed soldiers I entered into an air conditioned lobby that was too stuffy for my taste, but I asked the price for a room anyway. It turned out to be more money than I had on me. Then I wandered off in some random direction and found an unguarded hotel with a friendly staff, it had clean rooms with full bathrooms. I cleaned up and then walked around the blocks near my hotel. Representing Spanish influence was a bull fighting stadium, and representing other

---

[24]*$1.00 U.S. was worth approximately 5 lempiras.*

parts of the world was a Chinese restaurant, a Dunken Donuts, and M16s everywhere.

In the morning, on the way to the bus station, I saw dozens of small tanks, machine guns mounted in jeeps, various armored cars, and several groups of soldiers walking around. The ostensible reason for the show of force was to counter *delincuencia* (criminality). To a U.S. Peace Corps volunteer, who may not have been far off the mark, "The military is just showing who's boss," for a national scandal was unfolding, and something like demonstrations or rioting might have been feared.

The country's Human Rights Commissioner, Leo Valladares had just grabbed the ears of the country in a radio broadcast. He implicated members of the National Department of Investigation (D.N.I.) and the 3-16 Military Intelligence Battalion in the deaths of nine individuals and trafficking in narcotics, both in the country's booming industrial hub of San Pedro Sula -coincidentally my next destination. The backgrounds of the murdered (two were officially suicides) were mostly involved on the side of the law in the Narco War, a union leader, and a utility manager. Valladares' informant was former D.N.I. agent Josué Elí Zúniga Martínez, who was presently being sheltered by the country's Human Rights Commission. For the military's part, twenty-six year old Zúniga was "...perhaps in other aspects...(Zúniga) hasn't lied."[25] But the streets would be patrolled.

Regardless of whether the Narco War is blamed on demand for illegal drugs in the United States, or on drug

---

[25]From the English language Honduras This Week, vol. 6, num. 8, Tegucigalpa, Honduras, Saturday, February 27,1993. pp 1,2.

production in Latin America, and that it's true that Latin Americans lack subtlety in controlling people, the unfortunate fact for the Hondurans is that they are just a Molotov cocktail's throw away, or just a misunderstanding between soldiers and pedestrians, from a large scale war. Some nonviolent means must be employed immediately to end the Narco War, or Honduras, armed with new and improved ways of killing people, will become thoroughly bloodstained.

Traveling toward the old capital of Comayagua the bus passed the expanse of the U.S. military's Palmarola base. Perhaps this would have been the U.S. military's most important fortification had the U.S. invaded Nicaragua in the 1980s. All was new and shiny on the base, but the nearby old capital did not seem any better for the resident *gringos*, in fact, it was the most run down city that I saw in Honduras. The soldiers here were pink skinned, rather bumbling, unarmed and smiling, and there were several sexy women in red dresses around them.

On the bus I struck up a conversation with Michele, a Peace Corps volunteer from Minneapolis, and learnt several things about the organization. Judging from the conditions she lived in, her meager wage, and four years of service, she was obviously very committed to some higher ideal. But she was also cynical, and I think that her knowledge and beliefs are worth repeating, if not a book in itself. In Honduras there are about four hundred Peace Corps volunteers. They are primarily classified into medical groups, English teachers, economic development people, and "hillsiders" (agricultural consultants.)[26]

Michele feels that this is all fine, and that volunteers

---

[26]*These categories are, of course, very focused. I know from my own inquiries that people with history degrees need not apply to the Peace Corps.*

often do very good and useful work, but that many administrators are often more in the way than helpful; if they go out to field stations at all. One time she found out that her director had received a letter threatening to kidnap and kill volunteers in the area she was in; this tidbit took two months to reach her. Also, she feels that she's just a "political pawn," that is, when U.S. liberals point out how much profit U.S. companies pull out of Honduras, and how much money has been spent building the country's military, officials can point to the "humanitarian aid" entering the country in the form of the Peace Corps.

On the personal side she's experiencing a crisis in communicating with friends and family. The news from home is all about the new "Mall Of The Americas," where people can even spend their vacation at a shopping mall. Back home are baby showers and thousands of dollars are spent on the deceased, so that almost all people in Minneapolis can be kept in comfort from conception to eternity. Now, Michele works with a community trying to develop an economy for people that have been on a standard of living and political down-hill slide for untold generations, and no bottom is in sight. People back home have had their fill of her stories and emotions and what she tries so hard to say. Daily, Michele sees malnourishment, she knows corruption, she has seen young girls leave to entertain U.S. and Contra soldiers for a little money, and the reality that she suffers is less important to the folks back home than their trivial entertainments. College loans for volunteers can be deferred for four years, and now it's time for her to go home, get a job. I've never met anyone so scared to go to the United States.

The bus pulled into San Pedro Sula and it was immediately apparent that tensions were even higher here than in the capital, for this is where the latest scandal was centered. Troops were everywhere. The city of four hundred thousand is characterized by a Caribbean flavor, complete with black people, low altitude, and humidity. It also has a booming economy and a faster pace than the capital. I stayed one night but I had no special desire to linger. Guatemala, with a stop at highland Honduras' ruins at Copán, was calling.

After about five hours of travel by bus I was dropped off in the town of Copán Ruinas, where the pavements ends. The town is pleasant and uncrowded, and though it was as hot as San Pedro Sula, it was at least a dry heat. The main body of the area's famous ruins are only a short walk from town. On the roadside is a small museum and restaurant to serve tourists. Judging from the small parking lot, not too many people come here, but the entire area is clean looking, very mellow, and well maintained by the Hondurans. After several days of sprinting toward Antigua I was more than happy to stop here for a couple of days.

The ruins have been cleared of much of their forest cover since writer John L. Stephens, and his artist friend Frederick Catherwood, explored these ruins in 1839, but their work is integral to today's research at Copán. Many of the stelea, or "stone idols," had been carved by the pre-Columbian people here on a stone that is easily dissolved by rain water. Stephens and Catherwood, and various locals that they hired, removed the vines, roots and earth from several of the stelea. Stephens plotted their locations on a map, and Catherwood made precise drawings of the intricately carved face ornamentation, and hieroglyphics.

For a long time afterwards Copán again became covered in forest. However, since the present era's uncovering of the area for continued study, and tourism began, the intricate carvings have been weathering, and researchers today find Catherwood's drawings indispensable. Although Stephens and Catherwood were not able to decipher the hieroglyphics, these are now, in the last couple of years, beginning to be understood. Aside from some scattered examples of Ogham script, the writing system of the Celts, this seems to be the only pre-Columbian written history in the Americas, and it is, happily, much more revealing of Maya civilization than anyone had previously hoped to believe.

At dozens of sites in Mesoamerica we can now understand and be awed by the Maya's amazing calendrical system, read the dates of important events, the names of rulers, their beliefs about the universe, creation, and other worlds that are unseen but influence the daily life of those that we can see. Some of these legends were written on paper or deer hides, but most of these were either burnt by Spanish missionaries or decayed. Hidden in the jungles, though, the great stone stelea have awaited our day, and reveal to us the literature of a civilization that was apparently so traumatized by some as yet unknown event or process, that literatness pretty much disappeared by 900 A.D. I qualify the word "disappeared" with "pretty much," as it is possible that Mayas with knowledge of their writing system may well have been alive when the first Spaniards came to live among the Maya in the north of Yucatán. In fact, sixteenth-century Franciscan friar Diego Landa may have been taught, by Maya holy men, how to read the hieroglyphics; which he apparently found inflammatory, and commenced destroying the veritable Maya library that was at his hands.[27]

---

[27]*For more on friar Diego Landa see Inga Clendinnen's* Ambivalent Conquerors. *For Maya writing and calendrics see Linda Schele and David Freidel's* A Forest of Kings: The Untold Story of The Ancient Maya, *William Morrow and Company, Inc., New York, 1990.*

Some of the research going on at Copán is being done by U.S. university students. My superficial impression of the ruins, that is, the pyramids with their steps, the great walls, court yards, and especially the carvings and hieroglyphics, is that they were built by a highly organized and numerous people, and their leaders must have been learned. The ruins area cleared of forest is about two hundred meters squared, and there are several outlying ruins as yet unmapped and unstudied. No one knows precisely why centers like Copán were abandoned, but as will be seen in subsequent chapters, when I discuss my time among the Highland Maya of Guatemala, the descendants of the great builders, rulers, and intellectuals are currently in a state merely diminished, altered or adjusted, or suppressed, and the trace lives on in their culture.

A pickup truck stopped and gave me a ride, over the steep folds of the land north of Copán Ruinas, on the direct route to Guatemala. The border post is in a deep notch in a range separating the two countries. Gray clouds hung low. Mixed in with all the Central American travelers were several groups of backpacking travelers packed into beat-up V.W. buses.

In the 1960s it was in this area, the Eastern Highlands, that former Guatemalan army officers initiated a guerrilla war that goes on to this day. Within a few years, and after the government's brutal suppression of the area, killing all but combatants, the guerrillas moved on and emerged in other parts of the country.[28] Since then the Eastern Highlands have

---

[28] For a good summary of Guatemalan history, and the emergence of today's guerrilla groups that it has led to, see Jim Handy's Gift of the Devil, self copyrighted in Canada, published in the U.S. by South End Press, 1984.

been quiet, although recent activity suggest that conflict is brewing again. A couple of years prior, on this very road, guerrillas had stopped and searched buses, gave some lessons in Marxism, and "contributions" for the cause were accepted. I will discuss more guerrilla activity when I write about my second and finally successful attempt to reach Mataquescuintla.

Tree branches scrapped the bus as it splashed through streams where there were no bridges or culverts. This road would surely be impassible during the rainy season. Most of the steep land is covered in a wild forest, but there are small farms too. Many people rode horse and mules; a much more appropriate means of transportation here than a bus. In this rough land lives a Latino peasant society, much untouched by new technology and little seen by tourists. The culture is a blend of old Spain with this very locality.

After several hours the bus emerged onto the pavement of a highway and sped toward the city of Zacapa and the steamy valley of the Río Motagua. The land, though in its natural state might have been a jungle, is now an eroded desertscape of cacti and thorny plants. Bony cattle seek the few succulent plants. Ascending toward the capital the road twists with the ravines of the slope and trucks pass each other around blind curves with no respect for death. We crested a ridge and below lay the sprawling capital city of three million, beyond rose Volcán Agua and the ridge of Milpas Altas that I would cross to get to that most beautiful of Highland basins in which lays Ciudad de Santiago de los Caballeros de Guatemala.

XI.
Antigua Life

I arrived back at our hotel room at the Hotel Refugio, our place for one month, a day after Sean had left for Tikal and Cancún, México, by plane. In the latter he would meet Angie, for Spring Break, from Fort Lewis College. Subsequently he would do another one week trip to Livingston in the east of the country, and to Copán. Our room was narrow and had only one bed, which was fine since we only had to be there together for one night; that being the night that I arrived back from my infamous volcano expedition, when I was happy to sleep on the concrete floor, since I was at least near water again.

Upon Sean's return we rented a larger and more comfortable place. It had two beds, a large table and a couple of small ones, large windows opening onto a central court, and a clean bathroom across the yard. The best assets, though, were the people that lived there. Carlos was a school teacher and a radio disc jockey. Juan worked as an electronic repairman. Then there was the daughter and mother team of Cristi and Terri. Everyone was very nice to each other and we formed a sort of family, which at times included people that rented an empty room for a night. We were there for a month, and it was much better than the previous place.

Our tentative plan, after our two weeks in language school, was to have one person in Antigua at all times to be a base in contact with Professor Michael Fry. If something bad were to happen, one of us would always be able to contact Michael while trying to locate the other. Luckily we never had to use this foolproof rescue plan. Now it was my turn to be in Antigua. It would be at least a week before Sean would be back.

During this time I proposed to do research at the Archivo General de Centro America (General Archives of Central America) in the capital, a forty minute bus ride away, for which I hoped that my Spanish would be proficient enough to make it worthwhile. I also planned to see various sites in the capital. During this time, of course, I could not be all work, and so I joined the *Casa del Deportista* (House of Sport). There I worked out, and an added benefit was that it was one of the few places in Antigua where only Spanish was spoken.

Also to improve my Spanish, and to learn more about the region, I read a lot in Spanish, particularly short newspaper articles, which are convenient since it is conceivable to look up every word if necessary. In addition, I bought <u>Me llamo Rigoberta Menchú y así me nació la Conciencia</u> (English version, <u>I, Rigoberta Menchú</u>). This is not too good of a choice of book to learn Spanish with since it is written in a very non-polished Spanish, the way that many Indians speak it. Spanish is often merely a second or third language for them. But Menchú, the winner of a Noble Prize for this book, and her human rights and labor-activist efforts described within, gave me a feel for Guatemala's Indians and an urge to visit their communities. But this would come a little later.

It was almost *Semana Santa* (Holy Week), in the lead-up to Easter. Antigua is world famous for its celebration of *Semana Santa.* People fly in from Europe and occupy the expensive hotels. Many people also drive in from neighboring countries. The town becomes filled with tourists that come to see Antigua's brilliant processions and street *alfombras* (carpets).

A typical procession may involve hundreds of people. First, the course of the procession is prepared with elaborately designed *alfombras*. With countless shades of sawdust, colorful butterflies, vases of flowers, geometric designs, a leaping sail fish, scenes from Adam and Eve, and other symbols, are created. To make them more brilliant, and to keep them from blowing away, a light mist of water is continually sprayed on them through construction up until the time of the procession. Added can be the petals of millions of flowers, pine needles, and leaves laid out beautifully.

Multitudes line the streets. Their silence increases as the wailing sounds of horns and deep ominous drumbeats near. Around a corner comes a vanguard dressed in deep purple gowns, white belts of rope, and white turbans. They look very much like a Biblical populous of the Holy Land. The pace is slow, the mood solemn. The *alfombras* occupy only the middle of the street and the marchers file along on the outside. Then pennants and flags come into view. This is followed by copal smoke emitted from censers that are slowly swung on chains. The smoke is of a heavy, oily, sweet smelling nature. The atmosphere of Christ's imminent death increases.

Then the floats. The men carrying the floats are also dressed in purple gowns. Their sons march under the float with them; dressed in miniature gowns. Flanking them are spear and shield-carrying Roman soldiers in bright red capes and red crests over gold helmets and gold chest armor.

On the float, a statue of Jesus Christ is hauling his cross, while a thorny crown causes blood to stream down his face. A cardboard Holy City of Jerusalem is at his feet. Angels hover about. On one float the Devil is depicted leaping at Jesus, only to fall off the end of the float. The men carrying the float will walk on the *alfombras*, which destroys them. In this way a great sacrifice is made: The most beautiful and soft surface imaginable, made with loving care and great effort, sometimes two days in the making, becomes depressingly ruined; but it is worth it to comfort Jesus, for he struggles and suffers with the cross on his way to die for our sins.

Following are floats with the patron saints of the church sponsoring the procession. Women carry the Virgin Mary. The band of men in contemporary suits takes up the rear, and their sad music parallels the now smothered *alfombras*, representing Jesus's ordeal in the saddest book of the <u>Bible</u>, and tears flow down the faces of the people.

There are other ways of commemorating *Semana Santa*, and perhaps more interesting. Seeking to get some exercise, and away from busy Antigua for a day, I took a long walk through most of the small towns in the beautiful valley to the southwest of Antigua, between the three volcanos, and happened upon some surprises that were fairly inexplicable, a little scary, and thoroughly fascinating.

Before leaving, Carlos and Terri tried to talk me out of going on this walk by myself, saying that I would be robbed by Indians. I asked them to join me. They declined. It was a warm and muggy morning; robbers would certainly take today off. I took dirt back roads out of town. Tall trees shade countless rows of coffee bushes and cast their shadows over the road. In the village of San Lorenzo El Cubo there were farm animals of all shapes and sizes. The gardens that occupy all of every house's yard were freshly tilled and awaiting the approaching rainy season. I said a few *holas*, but there was almost no one around.

At the top of a ridge I viewed the little city of San Antonio Aguas Calientes. This place is known among foreigners interested in buying textiles, with complex Cakchiquele designs, but otherwise few foreigners come here. Something besides weaving was happening today, though. There was a mystical air about the place and the heavy smoke of copal was wafting through the streets and mixing with the humidity. The clouds darkened and the pre-noon seemed like dusk. Foot traffic from all the alleys moved toward a building on a narrow street. I followed.

Inside were huddled hundreds of Indians that must have come from the outlying villages, such as the nearly abandoned one I had passed earlier. They were there to pay their respects and make offerings to Jesus, whose likeness was reposed on a layout of flowers and leaves. Before him were piles of fruits and vegetables, galvanized buckets of water with live fish in them, and birds in cages. Statues of saints in elaborate costumes lined the walls. A chanting accompanied flutes and drums. A sort of village council sat behind the alter, dressed in purple and white gowns, and solemnly conferred. Everyone spoke softly in Cakchiquele, Guatemala's third most widely spoken language after Spanish and Quiché. People filed along past the body of Christ, crossed themselves, prayed, and moved on; the older ladies crying. Although I must have stood out, no one was either rude to me or acknowledged me in any way.

Outside lightning banged, wind howled, and buckets of rain flew inside horizontal every time someone opened the door. The storm passed in a few minutes, and I again set out on my walk. A nearly adjacent town is Santa Catarina Barahona. There the church was in shambles and covered in a spider web of scaffolding. At one time it sported a dome, which now looked collapsed, and the uneven appearance of the building's base and long cracks were the telltale signs of an earthquake. One day this mighty church would be repaired, but here, on the earth's "Ring of Fire," I had no doubt that it would fall apart again.

Onward I walked, through more coffee groves, on a little used road to Santiago Zamora. I almost missed it as it's up a side street from the main road and hidden by trees. The little village of four square blocks has an unmatched charm to it. All is in neat lines. The church is simple. Before it and to its side is open area. In the middle of everything is the village's covered water supply and clothes washing well.

The road to San Miguel Dueñas is a long straightaway. Although it was getting hot again the road is nicely shaded. The town square, just off dusty Highway Ten, is beautiful. Everyone was leaving though, as some religious event was winding down. In this town there were only a few people in Cakchiquele dress. Most people wore suits and dresses with as much dignity as they could in bare feet or old sandals. There was some discontent in the air and a dozen soldiers stood looking over the crowd.

From there I walked along wide and treeless Highway Ten in the splendid view of the three volcanos that I was now intimately familiar with, and I was getting to know the valley in between too. Here was a part of the world that was growing on me. I had taken trips, and to here I returned, and would continue to do so for several more weeks. Its sounds, smells, tensions, and beauty were becoming a part of me; it was becoming one of my homes, although physically temporarily, always in my heart. This feeling convinced me of the superiority of my mode of travel, and I felt bad for the tourists rushing around to see all and do all they could in a week or two. A case of malaria would be the best thing that could happen to a person like that. After walking some twenty-one odd kilometers I was back at Terri's "family hotel."

Since I was in my "home valley," I had the time to compare processions in two very different parts of the valley. In Antigua the very sophisticated designs of the *alfombras*, and the endless and elaborate processions through the colonial city dazzled everyone. Film manufacturers make a lot of money as the cameras of tourists never stop clicking, and camcorders hum. But was this just done for tourists? Certainly not, as the Antiguans pour out to take part in the events on their own, and their tolerance of outsiders make the tourists perfectly comfortable. But I wanted to see a procession without a lot of tourists around.

On foot is the only correct way to approach such an event, and San Antonio Aguas Calientes had touched me deeply. A couple of days later I walked there again and arrived just as one of their processions was starting. Here, like Antigua, there are *alfombras*, but unlike Antigua, these are of an infinitely more practical nature. They are narrow so that the people carrying the platforms with Jesus, the Mother Mary, and several saints, walk through the little city without actually stepping on the *alfombras*, but the statues on the platforms symbolically pass over the *alfombras*.

No one would want to walk on these *alfombras* anyway, as they are not of sawdust, but rather of vegetables and fruit, a roasted fowl here and there, buckets of fish, cages of birds, baskets of flowers, pine tree branches, framed photos and paintings, and collections of shells and crystals on coffee tables. Everyone's personal living room and alter must have been dragged out for the occasion.

The first time that I had passed through this little city I did not take my camera, as I really don't think it's a good idea to have a camera the first time you go somewhere. How can a person know a place upon a first visit? There cannot be any feeling put into a photo when there is no feeling, and this can only be gained with familiarity. So now I had my camera strung around my neck and I couldn't use it. I just stood there and took in all the sensations of the sights described above, the smell of copal, the sounds of crying and solemn singing and instruments. I was the only foreigner. Mine was the only camera. It was a very unfamiliar scene. I could not take a picture. Maybe next time.

During this period in Antigua I also traveled into the capital to see where one third of the country's nine million people live. It is in a valley and suffers weather inversions that trap air pollution near the ground, just as in Denver, Los Angeles, and Ciudad de México. In the capital I sought out the Archivo General de Centro América.

There I hoped to do research to back up my senior thesis, which I had done the previous semester in Durango. My thesis had been on the development of transportation in much of Hapsburg New Spain, that is, México and Central America from about 1521 to 1714. The idea was that, and still pending, that I would further my research toward the eventual possibility of a higher degree.

One of the primary conclusions of my research is that poor road networks parallel localization and disunity over wide regions, as is Central America's inheritance to this day. México, on the other hand, early on developed a far reaching and good road network, and, correspondingly, it is a large country today. In México this is partly because there were many valuable products, notably silver and gold, that required overland hauls, in varied terrain and climates, of hundreds of miles. Central America had some valuable products, notably cochineal (red dye) and indigo (blue dye), but these products were transported by mules that needed hardly a trail. Here, I am just mentioning the gist of my research so that the reader will have some idea of what I was doing in the archives. In the archives, difficult as it was for me to understand the colonial-era Spanish written in cursive, not withstanding my mediocre ability even in today's Spanish, I was able to find documents that backed up my earlier conclusions.

    My research aside, which is of perhaps little interest to most readers, one informative character I met there was Frantz Binder of Austria. In his mid-forties, trained in archival work in Europe, and in Guatemala for several years, his self-assigned task was to write a new guide to the archives. When I asked him how he earned money, he responded that he was "independent," and money, because so little was needed here, was not a problem. He struck me as a bit of an eccentric, but I suppose that a speaker of five languages has a right to be. When I am unsure about someone, especially in foreign lands, I settle back and watch how others treat the person in question. In Frantz's case, the archive's staff had complete trust in him. He alone, among the several people doing research there, was allowed to go into the large room containing the documents. The rest of us had to fill out several forms for each document that we wanted to see, then a staff member would go back and retrieve the material, whereupon we were watched.

    Over lunch with Frantz he told me a great deal about the archives. Most of colonial Spanish America's historical research is done in the cushy surroundings of Seville, Spain, at the enormous Archives of the Americas. But here, in rough Ciudad de Guatemala, is where the most significant, and least researched, materials pertaining to Central America rest. But they have not always rested peacefully. For instance, during the country's direct military rule, 1954 to 1992, it was not uncommon for figures in the military to barge into the archives and remove certain materials, particularly land titles. The loss is impossible to estimate. Also, just to intimidate intellectuals, in the national library, which is on the opposite side of the same building, soldiers did such things as haul out card catalogs and smash them up and set them on fire on the library's steps. I personally went and checked out the remaining card catalogs and found them in shambles, in need of physical repair, as well as being almost totally out of order. There are no computers or even modern typewriters anywhere in sight. Someone like Frantz, an intellectual with a great deal of tolerance for the Guatemalan research system, certainly has his work cut out for himself. In his home country of seven and a half million people, there are about four hundred and fifty professional archivists. Guatemala has one visiting volunteer archivist, that being Frantz.

Across the street from the library is a large park. At the far end is Guatemala's main cathedral. To the left is the Palacio Nacional, seat of government since 1943, built by dictator Jorge Ubico during his regime. The following year he was overthrown, partly because of the exorbitant amount of national wealth consumed in building the edifice. Today, after a quick bomb check, touring it is free.

It is constructed in a Spanish/Moorish design, typical of the south of Spain, but its exterior is of a Guatemalan green, and much of its art work is of New World influence. Its multi-floored architecture of column line hallways is open to the air on beautiful courtyards in the center of the building. In these are fountains, tall trees, and flowering vines ascend the columns for many floors. The sporadic striking sounds of typewriters emanate from offices along the outer perimeter of the building, but all seems pretty mellow.

The murals inside, over the two main entrances, captivated my attention for a long time. They beautifully depict Guatemala's history and many cultures, but they failed to convince me of any desire to bring about racial understanding, as México's murals do. Here they are not in a necessarily public place. Although it is open to the "public," most Guatemalans are so thoroughly uncomfortable with their authorities that they stay away. The halls were nearly empty both times that I visited the building. In this country, the colonial legacy of power and division by race, with a few notable exceptions, is still very much intact, as I will occasionally point out. In these halls that I walked, I had the feeling that the murals and beautiful architecture were for a ruling class's comfort, and for the consumption of visitors from rich countries.

Whereas government serves itself in Guatemala, on a bus ride to the capital I met someone who showed me another dimension of the country. Fifteen year old (let's call her) Maria was on her way to the capital to visit her brother, whom attends San Carlos University. When she was very young her parents were killed in Chimaltenango by soldiers. Now she lives in an "institute" (an orphanage) run by nuns in Antigua. She is very proud of the institute and invited me to come and see it. I went there and was very impressed. The institute has a music room, and all the girls play two or three instruments and practice singing every day. Maria speaks Spanish, Quiché, and Cakchiquele. Her classes are in math, writing, grammar and literature in all the languages she speaks, history, religions (both Catholicism and pre-Colombian faiths, as well as something of all the major world religions), and typing. She has traveled to the far corners of her country, and to El Salvador and Honduras too. The girls stay in religious facilities when they travel, and they visit historic sites, museums, and see cultural events. With her peers she seems extremely happy, and these young girls are watched with the eagle eyes of very protective nuns. These nuns are hospitable, but they never took their suspicious eyes off of me, lest I get any funny ideas with their little girls. Considering what had happened in Maria's earlier life, in the guidance of these nuns she will have a very solid foundation to build her life. The girls invited me to a concert for that night in Antigua.

Directly from the bar at the Rainbow I dragged along Miter, a German acquaintance of mine, to the concert. At the hall the girls flocked around me and Miter to welcome us - nuns spying from behind ferns. The girls sang adorably. Half a dozen boys from another orphanage played a marimba. During a break a couple of girls came and talked to me. They didn't have too many opportunities to talk to foreigners, but they were intensely curious about other countries, as well as what foreigners thought of Guatemala, and inevitably, how we felt about *religion*.

My answers to questions of doctrine were intentionally noncommittal. I certainly tried to have respect for the institution that was, I feel, providing so well for them.

I can think of few teenagers in my own country that have as much support, and are receiving such a well rounded education. On another bench sat Miter, and it was some time before I realized what was coming from the mouth of this tall, handsome, and well built blond, that had a dozen captivated and amazed girls around him.

Perhaps Miter thought he was still at the Rainbow, but out of his atheistic mouth came a steady train of anti-religious abuse. I had neglected to fill him in on who supported the girls, and what a fine job that they were doing. The last thing in the world that I wanted to see was dissention at the institute. Surely the girls would enter the wider world one day, and as many were destined for university, they would certainly come into contact with other beliefs. But now, I felt that they were a bit young, and very dependent on a specific religion that was, at any rate, doing a good job of bringing them up.

Later, I tried to reprimand Miter. I told him that making the girls discontent in spirit might not lead to good results, and that we were just outsiders that had no right to cause disturbances, especially religious ones for minors that depend on a religion to protect and raise them. I never thought that I would hear myself defending Catholicism, a religion that I had bowed out of several years before. Although I still have no intentions of realigning myself with any religion, in a place like Guatemala, I realized that the helpless must take help from wherever it is offered. I was also to have a taste of the secular school system.

As I have said above, Carlos, in the room next door, is a school teacher. All I knew is that the school was a one room affair of sixteen kids. I asked to tag along with him to see how a one room schoolhouse operates. I hoped to just sit in the back and listen. We left at 7:00 on his motorcycle, to the music of no muffler, over the rough cobblestone streets of Antigua and were soon in the countryside on dusty dirt roads. In San Cristóbal el Bajo we passed the area's high school, one of not too many in the country, where many of Antigua's privileged kids go to school. Beyond it we climbed a long switch-backing and dusty road to the ridge-top farming community of San Cristóbal el Alto.

There was one road with the houses right up to its edge. Carlos dodged a few chickens and goats and took me to see the beautiful view from the small soccer field at the far end of town. From its steep edge one can see the area's three volcanos. Carlos had been up Volcán Agua once, but never to the summits of Acatenango or Fuego. The latter was spewing more smoke than when I had been up there.

At the school, Carlos said *"Buenos Dias clase, este es Tomás. Adios."* Then he was gone. The kids looked straight at me. I looked out the door. I looked back at them. They were still looking at me. I forgot whatever Spanish I knew and *"Das ist gut"* (*Gm.,* This is good) came out. So much for lesson plans, I thought. I pulled myself together and went around the class to shake hands with each kid and we exchanged greetings.

I thought it would be a good idea to show them where I was from and how I came to be in their country. There were three maps in the class, one of Guatemala, one of the world, and one of North America.[29] On the latter map I showed them Colorado and described it a bit. I showed them the

---

[29]It is a common misconception that Central America is not a part of "North America." Geographically it is. It is a region that is as much a part of North America as is the Midwest or the Maritime Provinces.

approximate train route through México that I had taken, and the loop through El Salvador, Nicaragua, and Honduras that I had just recently traveled. The students could hardly believe it, most had scarcely been beyond Antigua.

Then it was map quiz time. Although my Spanish was still mediocre, the maps did most of the talking for me. Most of the little boys just sat there looking into space, as little boys do everywhere. But the girls got into our little game and they did very well. I decided upon a short walk to the soccer field, so that with the maps we could point in the directions of various places. The boys stampeded, the girls took my arms and hurried me along. Maps were our flags. Parents looked on confusedly, but approvingly. At the edge of the field I had them tell me what the three volcanos, and all the little villages were. Then, with the heel of my boot, I carved a large circle in the middle of the field. Having a good sense of direction (this has never kept me from getting lost,) I made it into a compass and we played our little game. Then I was told that it was time for recess.

I was dragged into a soccer game. Dust and the ball flew everywhere. Luckily the ball was very soft or a good kick in the direction of Volcán Agua (south) would have sent the ball a long way down the ridge. Exactly what the teams, rules, and boundaries were I don't know. I picked up a kid that was too good to get the ball from. I carried him around until his brother jumped me and the three of us went tumbling to the ground; then one by one kids fell from the sky and landed on the pile.

Back at the school, dirty but reinvigorated, I asked them if they would like to learn some English. They were unbelievably enthusiastic. We started with the ABC's. They would go along with me until near the end of the alphabet, then they would silence in order to hear me sing the last part (Now I know my...,) this always gave them a good laugh. They made me do it over and over again. Then it was time for the "other" recess. Two of the girls ran out and returned with a large pitcher of Kool-Aid. They rustled me up a tin and we had a little break, and I had to tell them the English names for everything around.

Carlos reappeared for the last hour and the class was decidedly more disciplined. Carlos' method was to quickly assign the oldest kids a task that would take them just enough time to give Carlos the chance to get the younger kids going on making letters or doing addition. It was an amazing juggling act. I sat in a little chair. With the youngest kids now busy, the sixth graders took turns reading aloud. Carlos called on me. I was looking out the window. The sixth graders giggled. But once I was on-line I did pretty good.

At noon the school day was done. The kids asked when I would be back. I had to hold back a knot in my throat as I said that I did not know. But I dreamt of coming back one day with a few presents and the school supplies that it looked like they needed. But I knew that it would be a long time until I returned, and that's all that would really matter, gifts or no gifts.

XII.
To the Continental Divide in the Department of San Marcos

With Sean, returned and tired from much successful travel, it was my turn to hit the road again. I went by bus and backtracked along the route I had come into Antigua as far as cold high Quetzaltenango. From there I determined to go directly west, instead of down to the steamy coastal plain from where I had come a couple of months earlier. The bus struggled up the paved but narrow highway and turned uncountable switchbacks. The route passes farms, as well as through forests of tall pine trees, on to the little city of San Marcos, the capital of the department.

This city is even higher than Quetzaltenango, and correspondingly cooler. Like much of the country's higher areas, the morning sky is usually blue, but by early afternoon fog rolls up the valleys from the Pacific and soon enshrouds everything, and that is how it was when I arrived in San Marcos. But the people have a sunny disposition, and the L.A. trained taxi driver delivered me to the pleasant Hotel Maya.

In the morning I was treated to the beautiful view of San Marcos in a valley nestled in the Continental Divide. Back in Antiqua I had managed to photocopy some sections of topographical maps of the two volcanoes that I wanted to ascend: Volcán Tajumulco, at 4220 meters ('13,862), is the highest summit in the country; and Volcán Tacaná, at 4093 meters ('13,385), is the country's second tallest volcano, and directly on the border with México.

The Continental Divide trends northwestward from San Marcos. Long sections of it are above 3,000 meters ('10,000). Though the Divide is crowned by patches of forest, for the most part it is farmed and grazed heavily at its summit and gently sloping Atlantic side. This has resulted in heavy erosion. Some corrective measures have been taken, but I doubt that the erosion has even come close to halting. An exciting bus ride follows the dirt road, which I shall call the Highroad, at the Divide's crest.

Toward the Atlantic, long stretches of highlands branch off the Divide, roads top them and lead to various towns that stand as islands in a sea of sky over the valleys. The main route to ascend this area leaves from the north side of San Marcos. All the routes from north and east of this highland northern part of the department are either four wheel drive routes, burro trails, or foot paths.

The volcanoes that I was interested in are to the Pacific side of the Divide. Long, steep and deep tropical valleys gash the land from the not so distant Pacific Ocean, right up to the Divide. All this high country would make for beautiful and endless backpacking trips, except that there is intermittent war in the department. On the coastal plains the Revolutionary Army of the Poor wages a war on unfair *finca* (plantation) owners that are backed up by the government's army. Now the fighting may be ascending the valleys, all the closer to the Divide. A new crop is reportedly being grown in Guatemala, and it is said to part of the reason that the fighting is spreading and becoming more vicious. This is cocaine. Perhaps it is the inevitable.

The <u>War on Drugs</u>, or, <u>The Narco War</u>, is a consequence of drug production, suppression, and use prevention efforts, primarily fostered by the Reagan\Bush White House, and continues. Although it is a current war, it is one of the least understood and poorly managed of all wars, yet it is arguably the most far reaching war ever to affect this hemisphere. Its turmoil engulfs in violence, cost people money, and promotes racism, from the cloud forests of Latin America, to the waters, sky, and roads of the hemisphere, and to the city streets and suburbs of the U.S. and Canada. By some accounts, it may even destroy democracy in the U.S.A.[30]

The growing of coca leaves, from which cocaine is derived, started as a legitimate activity thousands of years ago, and many thousands of miles from Central America, on the Amazon basin side of the Andean Mountains, but the Narco War has caused its production to spread. Production suppression efforts in Colombia, Peru, and Bolivia, has given growers incentive to plant elsewhere. It now appears that it has leapfrogged our boys at Panama and come to these Guatemalan valleys too, which certainly seem to be of a topography and climate similar to South America's Amazon Basin's rim.

All this posed a bit of a problem for me because I was worried that trouble from below, so close to where I wanted to go, might boil over onto the highlands. Furthermore, as I was to see, the larger towns of the highland area north of San Marcos are partly populated by what often seems a frustrated

---

[30]*For violence, the cost, racism, and extent, as well as a close look at the drug problem in one U.S. city, Washington, D.C., see Clarence Lusane, with contributions by Dennis Desmond's* Pipe Dream Blues: Racism and the War on Drugs, *South End Press, Boston, MA. 1991. For a clear discussion on the illegalities of the* War on Drugs, *and how it is threatening U.S. democracy, see Peter Dale Scott and Jonathan Marshall's* Cocaine Politics: Drugs, Armies, and the CIA in Central America, *University of California, Berkeley and Los Angeles, 1991.*

poor. The harsh living conditions lend themselves to alcoholism and fist fighting, which I saw there in abundance, and, I feared, robbery.

Dangers aside, I set off on a sunny morning. At the bus station I met Humberto, of Tacaná, a city at the end of the Divide's Highroad. He was to become an invaluable friend in an area so foreign to me as to be intimidating. A military construction crew was widening the road and placing culverts. Green bulldozers maneuvered around and guards stood the lookout. A roadblock of soldiers stopped us for half an hour. The usually impatient bus driver road-warrior resigned himself to the situation. Up and up and around hairpin switchbacks we went to the top of the steep section. There was a stone piled fortress with large calibre machine gun barrels sticking out of it. This is the gateway for most wheeled vehicles coming to the these high roads of the Divide, and until recently this was the only practical road to ascend the Divide.

One of the reasons that I came to this part of Guatemala was to discover a town, that is, a small urban area, that did not yet have a wheeled vehicle road to it, as many of the world's towns once were. This is related to my studies on transportation written about above. According to my maps, only a decade outdated, I should have been able to find such a town. But even here, in this rough country, bulldozers and tiers had beaten me by at least a couple of years. However, at least I was lucky enough to see some rural areas, even with considerable clusters of dwellings almost resembling towns, that were still inaccessible by wheeled vehicles, which I shall describe below.

From where there was a view I could see the fog

invading the valleys below and rising up until it eventually caught up to us and set everything in an eery gloom. It was early but it seemed late. The Highroad reaches the crest of the Divide at Cumbre (Pass) Tuichan. Here I got off the bus. A sharp right onto a road on the crest of a spur ridge leads to the small farms of Mam speaking Maya. Straight on the road, built about ten years previous, connects the Highroad with the little city of Tajumulco, some one thousand meters below. From there a road, only two years old, leads to the coastal plain, which makes this the only other practical route to these highlands. Curving and climbing to the right the Highroad leads to Ixchiguán and Tacaná, other roads branch off onto spur ridges toward other towns.

Here, at three thousand meters, the summit of Tajumulco was only six or seven kilometers away and twelve hundred meters above. But with the weather being as it was, and that I did not have a tent, I hesitated. Everyone was shy towards me, except for Domingo. No more than ten years old, he came right up to me, and in his Spanish, which was worse than mine, asked me what I wanted. I asked him if there was a hotel. There was none. His big brother Juan, twenty, then came to me and asked if he could help me. I asked if he thought it might rain. He said yes. It was cold, so I asked if it might snow. He said yes. I asked about the trail to Volcán Tajumulco. He offered a sweep of his arm at the slope across the Highroad. There, there was a random zig-zagging network of animal trails. I asked him if there was a place I might sleep. He pointed to his house.

Besides storage buildings and animal shelters, each farm consists of two buildings. One is the *sola*, used for sleeping. They are sturdily built, their walls are whitewashed, and their roofs are of thick wood shingles. Then there is the *cocina*, which is the kitchen. These buildings are made of thatch and mud attached to a wood framework. They have a lot of holes and are drafty, which is good because otherwise everyone inside would suffocate. There is no smokestack. A small smoldering fire burns pretty much perpetually. The smoke simply drifts about and escapes where it can. Its probably not very healthy, and everyone sniffles a lot (I had to sit near the door as I wasn't used to it), but it does serve a purpose. On shelves on the walls and over the ceiling rafters are stored sacks of food, mostly potatoes, corn, and vegetables. The smoke keeps rodents, insects, and fungus, from destroying the food. Black soot covers the entire inside.

    Juan's wife moved food about in the coals and sewed. Some of us where lucky enough to have miniature chairs; Domingo saw to it that I had the best one. There were about seven people living here, Juan, his wife, and younger brothers and sisters. Juan was the man of the house.

    Outside, I turned around and was hit in the face by a sewn together soccer ball. It barely held air. Domingo threw it. We started kicking it around in front of the *sola*. Other kids came and joined until we had to move across the Highroad to the bumpy soccer field. I started off as goalie. My strategy was to get out of the way every time someone came barreling down on me with the ball. This worked. It's a good thing that the ball held air so poorly, otherwise, a strong kick might have sent the ball down an endless slope. These kids, I think, had little contact with outsiders, and although they were intimidated by me at first, it soon wore off as I was doing such a poor job as goalie. Domingo didn't want to be on my team anymore. Once they were worn-out I took commend as a forward player and scored a couple of goals; Juan was my only real competition. I had returned Domingo's joke.

Before bed, Juan recommends that he guides me up the volcano, as I might get lost, and that their might be robbers up there. We awoke in the pre-dawn, went across the Highroad and ball field and up some steep and eroded slopes, trending southwest. Cresting the slope we came to an upland meadow with only a few scattered farm houses. In the distance there are trees, and the summit of Tajumulco looms gray and rocky. We pass tilled soil on steep slopes. Some crops are sprouting.

The sky is clear, but we know that we have many hours of walking to make the summit in time to still have a view, as the afternoon fog will roll in. The lower forest has no lower branches, and there are many stumps. The fuel for cooking in the highlands is wood and the forest is paying for it. In 1965 there were four and a half million people in Guatemala, now there are twice that number. In light of this I don't see that the already overtaxed forest will be able to supply cooking fuel indefinitely. Here too there are more people. My 1970 topographical maps show all the rural houses that stood then, but it's seriously outdated as it does not show half the houses that stand now.

The fields are eroded to varying degrees. In places the grass cover and topsoil are well intact. In other places there are gullies as much as two meters deep and ten wide. These sometimes form intertwined mazes leaving only mesa-like islands of rich soil covered by grass. Yet other areas are moonscapes of lose jagged volcanic rock or smooth surfaces of bedrock.

I breathe hard in the thin air but it feels good to be at some altitude. A half kilometer ahead of us are three other hikers. The short man in front is obviously the Guatemalan guide, and I judge his clients to be a male and a female German, for their erect solid walk and duffel bags over one shoulder are a sure giveaway. We catch up to the other party and sure enough they are from where I guessed.

The Germans are looking pale and drinking out of glass bottles of mineral water. The five of us carry on. Juan and the other guide, form the town of Tajumulco, lead and talk away in Mam; probably making fun of us tourists. These guides wear beaten up formal dress shoes with no socks. We foreigners wear much better gear but are not better hikers. At tree line we stop for a long break. Now we are only two hundred meters from the top and the route turns steep and full of boulders to negotiate around and over. The Germans are looking especially white and exhausted. Their guide calls them on but I tell them to relax and insist that they drink big gulps of my water, as I have plenty. They are from Bavaria, but its highest mountain is only 2,800 meters high. When they start to look a little better I teach them my strategy of taking two steps then pausing, two more steps then pausing. It is slow, but what is important is that it is a pace that the legs and heart can maintain a rhythm to.

  First we ascend the lower summit, which has a view of the town of Tajumulco in a valley two thousand meter straight below. I ask the other guide about when the roads, which were not on any of my maps, were built, and this is how I obtained the outline of when these roads were built, which I related earlier. But Tajumulco is still off the main paths, the Germans, like me in Tuichan, are the only foreigners in our towns. They like Tajumulco very much.

Juan and I wished the others well and set off for the summit, which forms a part of the rim of the volcano's crater. Finally we arrive at the top of Guatemala! The crater is about seventy meters (210 feet) in diameter and its floor is fifty meters (150 feet) below the highest part of the rim. A few clouds start to build around the mountain, and the Pacific Ocean, otherwise easily visible, is obscured by haze. We descend to a pass and ascend Tajumulco's lower sister peak, Cerro Concepción. According to a guide book it is used for "Shamanistic rituals," but I think that that is just exciting hype, for I did not see any signs of offerings or burnt areas, only a beautiful rocky outcropping.

On the descent we pass flocks of sheep wreaking their destruction to the grass and soil, pulling up roots and all. There are horses, goats, and cows too. The clouds start to roll in and we hurry down. We arrive at Juan's house before noon, but the fog is already so thick that it seems much later. I thank them all for their hospitality, pay Juan a guide fee, and am just in time for a bus to the little city of Tacaná.

On the road, although only about thirty-five kilometers (twenty-two miles), it still takes over three hours to get to Tacaná as it is dirt and rolls along near and on top of the Divide. We climb and descend through a protracted series of switchbacks. It's probably Guatemala's highest road, with altitudes from San Marcos to Tacaná usually between 2,500 and 3,600 meters.

To the Pacific side it is steep and mostly forested. On the Atlantic side it is less steep and used heavily for crops and grazing. This side is also heavily eroded, even worse than on the slopes of the volcano I have described above. Fortunately, some check dams have been built in gullies, some terracing has been done, and a few small tree farms dot the land. Although the fog is thick, it sometimes opens up and provides beautiful views of distant ranges and valleys.

Along the way I saw many people, and, sadly, I might add, almost all their clothing looked as though it had been donated by U.S. charities. The names of many U.S. sports teams and companies were written on them. All was soiled and falling apart. As this area is so far from the main tourists centers of the country, I was really surprised and disappointed to see that so few, usually only a woman here and there, wore clothing of Indian design. I wondered how many local weavers have been put out of business by the good intentions of people getting rid of what they would not wear themselves. An Indian in Indian clothing always looks sharp, in Western design they sometimes do not.

In Ixchiguán the main road was blocked off for a fiesta. Looking down that road all looked like a chaotic drunken mess. We took a steep detour. All the passengers had to get out of the bus to lighten the load, but even then the bus barely made it up the hill. Even on the back streets people staggered about. Two guys were fighting. They swung wildly but usually missed, thanks to their opponent falling down or something. The punches and kicks that connected lost their snap in the alcohol. The town was pathetic.

In Tacaná I took a room for Q4. (about .75 U.S.). It was not a bit overpriced. My room was a box on the second floor. A ladder led to the walkway above the courtyard. The room was furnished with a dirty bed. But that was tolerable since I always used my sleeping bag. I was under the impression that this was the only hotel in town. Out on the street things were hardly better. Tacaná's streets are narrow, chaotic, and dirty. Hawkers speak with megaphones advertising vitamins while holding up photos of the starving children that did not have the benefit of their products. Many people looked on and listened seriously at the sincere sounding salesmen.

People looked at me strangely as they were unaccustomed to strangers. Then I saw Miriam, Humberto's sister. In the mess of Tacaná she's an island of loveliness. Her clean white dress is in contrast to her surroundings. We had spoke for a long time on the bus ride from San Marcos to Cumbre Tuichan, where I left her, Humberto, and their mother. Miriam is sweet and pretty and only sixteen. She was showing me to a restaurant when Humberto and his friend Rony showed up. They joined me. Now I did not feel so all alone in Tacaná. Whereas before, since I was obviously rich to the people of this town, it must have followed to them that I wanted something from their neighborhood that I was too ashamed of getting in my own neighborhood. Several shady looking guys wanted to talk to me, they wanted to be my "guide," or to see if they could help me buy something. But now they avoided me as I had the credibility accorded to people with other people.

I took leave of Miriam and went off with Humberto and Rony. Rony is from San Marcos and worked in the office of a construction company that was doing work in Tacaná. Humberto is a machinist in Tacaná. They knew each other from work, and they attended the same evangelical church. They quizzed me about many things. Rony asked if it was true that all girls in the United States are *rubias* (blonds) and beautiful. I explained to him that not all *rubias* are pretty, I knew some that are fat and ugly, while all the pretty ones are taller than Rony.... That was just a warm-up question though.

It was their dream to go to the U.S. There they hoped to be able to earn amounts of money that most Guatemalans would not dream of making in Guatemala. Rony had twelve years of education, including one at a university, and Humberto had nine years. Both are lucky, in the villages along the Divide, such as Tuichan, most people only receive three years of schooling. In the little cities, such as Ixchiguán and Tacaná, six to seven years is the usual.

I hope that I gave them good advice on preparing to come to the U.S. I told them to learn English as well as possible, talk to as many people as possible that had been there, get addresses of people related to friends up there, try to get documents together such as a passport, apply to colleges and universities (particularly in Rony's case) as these can be good entrance cards, have excuses for crossing into the U.S. and being there, and most of all to have a lot of money in traveler's checks; I recommended at least $1,000. I also told them to expect to take at least two years to complete all my preparations -Humberto was ready to leave with me in three weeks, with only Q400. ($80.00).

On the other hand, I suggested that perhaps the U.S. was merely a symbol for them, as it is with many people from countries like Guatemala. I cautioned them that immigrants to the U.S. were often disappointed, and that moving there did not always improve lives. If they do come to the U.S., of course, I will help them in whatever way I can.

Later I went with them to Humberto's house in the *colonia* (suburb) of Los Angeles. In front of the house there is a large garden, and like Juan's home in Tuichan there are two main buildings, the *sola* and the *cocina*, only Humberto's house, being in town and claiming not to be *Indigena*, but *Latino*, was more luxurious and modern. For instance, it has a concrete floor.

His mother was very kind and served me coffee, with a lot of sugar, as is their way. I asked her if things had changed much in Tacaná in her life. She confirmed this and said that the biggest and best change was the new road connecting Tacaná with San Marcos. It had only been open for about twenty years, and now people could come and go any time they wanted to. She recalled that coming and going used to require many days journey, and people rarely left. I could not imagine that the road I had traveled to get here, on the crowded bus, would be considered an improvement by anyone. The old days must have been tough. Maybe it was harder on some than on others, though. Perhaps today's truck and bus drivers are yesterday's mule herders. Phones had not reached Tacaná.

In the morning, with Humberto's help, I found another hotel. This one cost Q5. and it was a great step up. It was clean and there was a shower with hot water! As it was Sunday there was an incredible market in the streets. Walking anywhere takes a lot of time. With Humberto I wonder around. I pay for the *refrescos* (pops) and I teach him some English. He teaches me some Spanish and introduces me to people.

One guy Humberto introduced me to spent five months *"en la cárcel"* (in the jail) in Denver. In all that time he did not learn any English. I asked him why he had not learnt English there. He asked me whom he might have spoken to in the jail to learn English from. He said that half the jail's guests only speak Spanish, and none of the non-Hispanic guests would speak to Hispanics. I asked if it had been difficult for him to cross into the U.S., he said no. I asked if he felt discriminated against in the U.S., to this he answered yes. And now here he was, free and in Tacaná.

I asked another man about wages. He said that in Tacaná he could earn Q10. for a day's labor, when work was available. Traveling to the Pacific lowlands of the Sosconusco coast in México one might earn a little more and convert it to Q12. The nearest Mexican *fincas* are over one hundred kilometers away, over rough roads or trails. When people go to those unhealthy places of malaria and hard work they stay for several months at a time. *Fincas* on the Guatemalan Pacific coastal lowlands pay even less.

That evening Humberto and Rony came and got me to go to church with them. Rony was in love with sixteen year old Patricia Elisabeth, the daughter of the hotel owner, so it was difficult to get him moving toward the church. From down the street, walking with Humberto, in English I yelled a few choose remarks back to Rony, and urged him to follow.

The church, Monte Sion, was a little building with a few pews and a podium with a chalkboard behind it. The paster was scarcely twenty-five, but he spoke well and had charisma. His wife kept everyone's children in an attached building. Three men played guitar to our audience of about twenty people. I sat with Humberto and Rony, and Miriam and her friend Sandra.

In front of us was a talkative drunk. I was ready to throw him out at the start but opted to wait and see how the Guatemalans would handle him. There was singing and readings and drawing on the chalkboard -the church doubled as a school. During the singing the drunkard usually couldn't find his hands for clapping, but his voice was more or less in harmony. During readings he shouted out several times and he was warned *"Esta es una casa de Dios"* (This is a house of God) a dozen times. Meanwhile, other people that were attracted by the singing came to the gated entrance and stared inward. Several of the men seemed intoxicated and there were retarded looking children, too. One of the well dressed regulars would always invite them in and show them to a seat. The kindness and tolerance demonstrated was incredible, but the drunkard before us had to be ushered out the door halfway through the one-and-a-half hour service.

A hat was passed around for the collection. This accomplished, the money was counted by the pastor and his eyes rather lit up. He announced the sum collected, and to my amazement, I had contributed four-fifths of the total; and I thought that I had given so little. Everyone kind of knew it was me that put in the hefty amount. But I wasn't in the least bit regretful, as I knew that the money would be well spent. Toward the end of mass special thanks was given to me for my visit, and a prayer was said for me to protect me on my proposed hike up Volcán Tacaná, and on all my travels.

But not everyone in Tacaná had attended church. On the way back to my hotel there was a crowd of people blocking the street and making a circle around six to eight guys that were fighting. The audience was very drunk and laughed and cheered and clapped when one boy did a bunch of clumsy karate kicks. The darkness was lit up by the lights of a Toyota pickup—there was a power outage. There were also people shouting from rooftops and monkeyishly swinging from electric poles; at this I thought Tacaná's a veritable stadium of gladiators, and wrote the following poem:

Weekend in Tacaná

Traveling to coastal *fincas*
to do slave labor
and humiliation
drives them north
to the U.S.
to hide like rats
from the law
and then to be
put into
la cárcel (the jail)
just for being
in the U.S.
or maybe
for doing some petty crime
'cause they gotta eat
as they're being
cheated at work
and taken advantage of
and know it.
. . . .
So here they stay
on the Continental Divide
in Tacaná
high
on eroding slopes,
depleting forests,
poor education,
unsanitary conditions,
alcoholism,
underpaid,
and tearing at each other
from Friday afternoon
to Sunday night.

Yesterday I missed the bus (literally) from Tacaná to the turnoff for Sibinal, which is just to the Pacific side of the Divide. It didn't look like hitching would turn out, so when a guy offered to take me there for Q50, I took him up on it. Another guy going the same distance, who got in when I did, gave the driver only about Q3. I was angry and thought it should be split. We settled upon Q40. for me. I was steaming with humiliation until I took a few steps to the crest of the Divide.

Over the rim of the Divide was a forest of huge trees and the view was of a huge caldera of a valley, with Sibinal at the center, and all very symmetrical. Walking down the road a ways were a man and a woman relaxing by a waterfall. They confirmed that it was clean water and that there were no houses above. I drank heartily and washed a bit.

I shook hands with the several other people along the road and waved and said *"¡Buenos dias!"* to many others. The area was beautiful and there wasn't much litter. I had finally found the idyllic Latin America I had been looking for. I bought food at a little *tienda* and received directions from twenty or so men and boys gathered around to see this *extranjero* (foreigner.) A military man came to talk to me, too, his two buddies stood off a ways. He just wanted to know what I was doing. Satisfied that all I wanted to do was to ascend Volcán Tacaná, he let me pass.

I set off for the switchbacks to the top of the caldera-like valley's rim. From their the trail skirts three knobs and sometimes has very steep drop-offs. I arrived at La Haciendita and asked the lady at the first farm for a roof to sleep under, she pointed to the storage shed. La Haciendita is in a broad col and cleared of trees. There are about four families. *Milpas* were being planted. I arrived there in a dense fog. A son of the family took me down a slope to a nice spring. Technology failed me though, as my water filter stopped working. Toying with it I slipped on some rocks, I must have looked pretty clumsy to this boy. Finally I drank straight from the spring and it tasted great; perhaps getting away from the iodine resin in the water filter was good for me.

I took a much needed nap. I woke up when Roberto, the father of the house, got back from working in Sibinal. He works grain in Sibinal, and raises potatoes in La Haciendita. He has three daughters and two sons. His oldest son has been in the U.S. for four years, and is now in Atlanta doing carpentry. Roberto went there too with four buddies and worked in Maryland. He spoke English quite well, yet his Spanish was worse than mine. He liked the U.S., he had good experiences there, and he liked his job on a poultry farm.

His family seemed very happy, as did everyone else that I met in the area. War in the 1970s and 1980s had totally missed this area. Up here away from roads there are no cars, no electricity or phones, but many people do own radios. These they often played tied to a horse while commuting to and from Sibinal; for a while I hiked to Olivia Newton John!

I was up at 6:00 A.M. and headed up the trail. Whoever drew the trail on the map must have been dreaming. I ended up bushwhacking a long steep slope of 1,000 meters. I reached the top of a knoll and had a fine view of the summit in clear blue sky. The rest of the way was a combination of run-out trails and bushwhacking. Near the top one enters a crater that has another cone in it. On top of this inner cone is the summit.

There are trees almost to the top, but trees give way to boulders and rocks that make a perch for a fine view toward Volcán Tajumulco, and the deep lush valleys in between. Beyond Tajumulco are other volcanos piercing the clouds. Westward into México a bank of clouds covers the south rim of the Chiapan highlands. The Pacific is too hazy to see. Northward, the town of Tacaná perches on a ridge above a river. Beyond is the high tableland of the Cuchumatanes. To the north and east stretches the Continental Divide. On the

Mexican slope of Volcán Tacaná, a few hundred meters down the slope, is a sulfurous gas being pumped into the air. Its scent wafts upward toward me. I enjoy the sun on a nearly windless day on the summit and take pictures of the green lizards scurrying about the rocks. There are also birds and butterflies. There is a wrought iron, broken funeral cross to remind me that it can be dangerous up here.

With clouds encircling the lower slope of the mountain and rising quickly, I head downward and hope for a better route down than I had upwards. Fifteen hundred meters down I run into the fog but I am comforted to know that I am at least in familiar territory and on the correct side of the mountain. If it had gotten foggy when I was at the summit, directions may have been a problem as I had forgotten my compass. I see two Indian women tending sheep and goats in a forest meadow, they point me in the direction of their community, which has a trail to La Haciendita.

The community is a scattered group of thatch roofed huts and lean-tos on a steep-terraced hillside, and surrounded by nature. Clouds revealed and then closed views of distant ridge top and hillside communities like this one. There is no distinct trail so I make my way down rock retaining walls and across the mostly unplanted fields. Walls were anywhere from one to two meters tall. People were very friendly and directions consisted of a vague pointing downward and a sweeping gesture to bear left.

I could not believe how people lived there. Their lives cling precariously to the hillside. There were none of the bothers of cars, and it is not hectic, but they had plenty to do and to worry about. The dry season spring was a kilometer away, but at that distance it was for drinking and not irrigation. At any rate, if it were used for irrigation, there would not be enough water for all to use. So they relied on rain and moisture laden fog. Too much rain might cause a landslide and sweep them thousands of meters downward into the *barranca* (canyon) below. Crop failure of any kind would be a disaster for these people. Earthquakes happen often here, too, although I never felt one. The dangers that the people face are basic, unpredictable, and merciless. One man had only one leg, I thought that this was a hard enough place for people with two legs. But, here, in compensation was independence, the dignity derived from self-reliance, and a beautiful view.

At La Haciendita, where I had left most of my stuff, I packed and headed down the trail. It wasn't raining, but the fog was so dense that it clung to pine needles and dripped off so that it was raining under the trees.

Back in Sibinal I took a bed in a pension, sharing a room with about six other people, and waited for the bus to depart at the ungodly hour of 2:00 A.M. It was a long cold night ride, but from the Divide the view was of an illuminating sky gradually turned red, then orange, and then yellow, white, and blue. We reached the military post at the top of the switchbacks and started down off the Divide to the valley below and San Marcos. Where the road narrowed a truck coming up was stuck, so we had to get out and push it up before we could continue downward. Near San Marcos an irrigation ditch spilt water onto the road. This made for a slick surface that our bus slid on and into a ditch. Forty or fifty men, from our bus and two others, redirected water, shoveled dry sand under the tires, and we moved on again, each in our own pursuit.

XIII.
The Capital and Mataquescuintla

Back in Antigua it's good to see Terri, Cristi, Carlos, and Sean again. Sean's conducted several impressive recorded interviews, as was one of our projects for our college credits, and has done extensive research at the National Archives. His Spanish has improved to the point that I'll never catch up to him, but he's lovelorn for his fiancé and ready to go back to Colorado. I talk him into staying a couple more days so that I can have company while wandering around the capital.

We take the half-hour bus ride to the capital. For Sean, the very essence of Guatemala is mirrored in these buses. This is not without reason. Only three percent of Guatemalans own a vehicle, but everyone travels and it's on these buses that they do so. Bundles of products for and from markets are hauled on the roof racks, the people crowd inside. Drivers hate to leave without an overstuffed bus. More people is more money. Their assistants run around howling the destination in abbreviated form, *"¡Guate! ¡Guate!"* or *"¡Huehue! ¡Huehue!"* or *"¡Quetzal! ¡Quetzal!"* while the engine revs up and the bus lurches forward in mock takeoff.

This is a little game designed to make prospective passengers think that this bus is leaving now, and it's the last or only bus. All the passengers get annoyed at the long time it takes to really get rolling, and you don't leave until the bus is infuriatingly overcrowded. Everyone steams, but they resign themselves to the situation once the bus is finally moving. The drivers are all road-warriors. They love nothing better than to have cute girls sitting behind them or on the control panel between their seat and the left window - there are no woman bus drivers. The assistants can be cordial or rude. But it is the good disposition of the passengers that make these rides at all tolerable- and this is really how the whole country operates: lots of false starts, little lies, under facilitated, and good natured people that can take a lot of abuse. However, Sean really does believe that if driver and assistant were to push the limits of their position, that of the purveyors of transportation, too far, the passengers would errupt into a mutinous army and commandeer the bus and make driver and assistant walk. And this, in microcosm, is Guatemala.

In the capital we breakfast at the cleanest and most modern McDonalds that either of us had ever seen. We tour the Palacio Naciónal, the Cathedral Metropolitana, and take a bus to the north end of town to see the Mapa Naciónal. This last attraction is my favorite. The map covers about an acre and there are two viewing platforms. It is made of concrete and shows all the cities, highways, rivers and mountains of the country. I can identify the five volcanoes that I've hiked to the top of, they are five of the country's six highest. Until a few years ago this would have been an "illegal map," and that is why Belize is included, for only recently has Guatemala dropped its claim to Belize.

The next day Sean left Antiqua for Durango, and I for Mataquescintla. This takes me through the capital again and to a very poor section. In the city center I ask directions to the necessary bus stop. People warn me not to go there. I go anyway. Once there I stand on a rise and before me is a sea of tin roofs covering shanties and small businesses. On the ground is litter and the scents are many and unpleasant. People tell me to be careful. I ask for the bus to Mataquescintla. No one has heard of Mataquescintla. They are sure that I want Escuintla, and tell me that I am in the wrong place. I insist and I ask around some more. Finally I meet a man that knows where Mataquescintla is and he directs me to the correct bus.

The driver's assistant is cleaning the bus and is sure that I'm mistaken, but, if I want to ride anyway, we'll leave right away. About six hours later we depart the noisy city. The road crosses a bridge over a gorge, in the cliff walls are tunnel entrances were people live. At the bottom are more tin roofs. The bus climbs above the slums and passed mansions with views of the capital below.

It's dark soon and the pavement runs out. The road is carved out of steep hillside and narrows to one lane. We climb upward into the eastern highlands, there are a few faint lights in the valley far below. We descend a mountain and splash through a stream as wide as the bus is long; good thing it's still the dry season. As the bus ascends another mountain it rounds a curve and there's two huge headlights beaming at us. The truck cannot back upward, so the bus slowly backs down a couple of hundred meters to a wider area. Intelligently, our driver pulls to the hillside, while the truck floats by on the airside. The bus continues and we arrive in Mataquescintla at ten o'clock. I take a room in a pension.

Walking around Mataquescintla I immediately realize that it's different than any other place I had seen. It's a real Latino, remote, perpetually frontier town. Most of the roads are dirt, while a few have cinder paving stones. It's friendly enough and casual. The church is large but not fancy. There's some building going on and it looks like there's some new buildings since Michael Fry was here. His objective in being here was to study land tenure records to determine whether people were able to hold onto their land with the country's independence from Spain in 1823.

His conclusion is that with the switch from conservative "monarchist" policies, to liberal economics, is that most small landholders were not able to retain their lands. Part of the significance of his work is to demonstrate what may be a stable and beneficial economic model, versus an economic model that fosters a greater concentration of wealth and accompanying social instability; the scale of which is probably Latin America's greatest problem today, and this disparity is greater now than during much of the colonial period.

The colonial period represents a kind of Golden Age for Latin America. Certainly the Spanish Empire of the sixteenth through nineteenth centuries was one of the largest, one of the longest lived, one of the richest, and if not efficient, then at least effective, empires that the world has ever seen. An example of the kind of place that the Spanish Empire was can be seen in the ghost ruins of Antiqua.

Michael's choice of working in Mataquescintla was partly because its very remoteness has left its archival records well intact; Mataquescintla has been overlooked. In fact, it cannot even remember its own past, that is, this was the home of Rafael Carrera, the holder of real power in Guatemala from 1838 to 1865, one of the country's most effective and popular rulers in the post independence period. From here, Carrera lead a successful peasant assault on Ciudad de Guatemala. Carrera was a rough and tumble and illiterate swine herder, but he was intelligent, charismatic, and had a violent temper. However, there is no statue of Carrera in Mataquescintla, and, in fact, when I asked questions about him, no one had ever even heard of him.

But the area has not stopped producing brave people,

for here, in the 1960s, is where the first guerrilla armies rose to take on the country's military. Although those earlier movements have been suppressed, fighting still goes on, and the issue has not changed. When I was there, there were soldiers in the streets, M16s slung over there shoulders. Curiously, all these soldiers were of very light skin, and one of them was a woman! Both of these traits are unusual in comparison to all the other Guatemalan soldiers that I saw. Eerily, too, the seven or so soldiers that I saw all turned and moved away from me when they saw me. Rounding the corners of buildings they looked back over a shoulder toward me. Of the fighting, from what I could gather, ten kilometers east of town, one hundred and fifty *guerrilleros* (guerrillas) had the main road blocked off and had forcibly taken back lands that they had lost to a large company, a cattle company, I think.

  This was to interrupt my plans. One of the things that I wanted to do in Guatemala was to visit one of its great lakes, for which the country is famous. Lago de Atitlán, set in a massive caldera and surrounded by volcanoes, would be easy to get to, but from all that I have heard about it, it is one big tourist trap, and for that reason I decided not to go there. However, and conveniently, Mataquescintla -of all places,- just so happens to have Laguna de Ayarza only fifteen kilometers to its southeast. This lake, also in a caldera, would substitute nicely for Lago de Atitlán, less all the tourists. I had planned to walk, or to get there by whatever means I could find (Michael Fry had visited the lake on horseback), however, with fighting only a short ways off, I lost nerve and decided to see it another time.

XIV.
The Cuchumatán Highlands

Although apprehensive about the long journey home, I was also looking forward to getting back to Durango and graduating, however, there was just one more corner of the country that I wanted to delve into, the Cuchumatán Highlands, or the Cordillera de los Cuchumatanes. From Antigua I took a crowded bus to Chimaltenango, then a luxury bus to Quatro Caminos, the next ride was in the back of a dump truck. As people climbed in or out of the truck they walked up to the driver and handed him some small amount of cash. When I got out at Huehuetenango,[31] I went to pay the driver, but, as in Nicaragua, the ride was a *regalo* (gift). I thanked him and went into town.

Huehuetenango is the capital of the department of the same name, the central park of the city is small, but it is one of the nicest in Guatemala. It is surrounded by the main buildings of the department. In the park there is a three dimensional concrete map of the Department of Huehuetenango. On the map, as in the view, the Cuchumatanes tower boldly over Huehuetenango. There are none of the symmetrical volcanic cones as are found parallel to the Pacific coast, for the Cuchumatanes are a high tableland formed of limestone. From Huehuetenango the Cuchumatanes appear to be a high flattish ridge. The tableland is as high as the Continental Divide in the Department of San Marcos, but the Cuchumatán high area is far more vast.

---

[31] *Pronounced Way-way-ten-an-go.*

Huehuetenango is a Latino city, but milling about and come to trade or work are many Maya from the Highlands. Those from the town of Todos Santos Cuchumatán are especially noticeable, for they proudly wear their traditional outfit of red stripped pants and a bowler like hat. Todos Santos Cuchumatán is Guatemala's highest community, and the special adaptations that they have devised to live up there have attracted many anthropologists and tourists. Today, a Spanish language school in Huehuetenango has a branch school in Todos Santos Cuchumatán, where students live with Maya Cuchumatán families, and therefore also learn a little of a Mayan tongue. This new institution is a laudable addition to the town's economy of weaving, herding, and terrace agriculture, but things have not always been so good in Todos Santos Cuchumatánt.

In the early 1980s, Todos Santos Cuchumatánt, like so many other rural communities in Guatemala's Western Highlands, was subjected to the terror of the army looking for Communist guerrillas, which were never very numerous in the area. Many innocent people were killed, while tens of thousands fled to refuge camps in México. We may never know the extent of the damage. Certainly rural life was greatly disturbed, and Indian distrust of Latinos worsened.

Before heading up into the highlands I visited the ruins of Zaculeu. Situated between two ravines, it was difficult for the Spaniards to conquer from the Mam Maya. Zaculeu was the center of Mam culture in the Post Classic Maya period. The more famous Maya sites of Tikal and Copán had already yielded to the jungle and forest, but Zaculeu was still a viable political, cultural, and economic center in 1524. The main area of ruins is several hundred meters squared. There is one pyramid of about three stories, a ball court, and several other buildings and small pyramids. The site was conquered in 1524 when Gonzalo de Alvarado laid siege to Zaculea and a bloody one month battle ensued. But, like victory over the Quiché earlier that year, this was only one of an endless string of confrontations.

In Huehuetenango I met several foreigners on their way to Todos Santos Cuchumatán. I was intending to go there, too, but then I saw a sign that read, in English: Todos Santos Bus Station. In Colorado I get enough of the tourist industry, I knew that Todos Santos would have to wait for another time for me. So I determined to go to more obscure places, Soloma, and San Mateo Ixtatán, toward the northern edge of the Cordillera de los Cuchumatanes.

The bus switchbacked forever upward until we crested the rim of the tableland. On the rim were limestone fangs jutting out like cannons pointing at the lowlands. Later the road passed through more limestone and there were dozens of catchments to conduct water to vertical cave shafts, thus accounting for this moist area's scarcity of ponds and streams. In places there was low relief karst topography, that looked, especially with the fog wafting around, like a Devilish landscape. I am sure the evangelizing Dominican friars of the sixteenth and seventeenth centuries thought these areas to have been terrain expurgated from hell.

Most of the land, on the main tableland of the Cuchumatanes, is given over to crops or sheep grazing, and there are some tree farms. The land is divided up by tall stone walls. The bus came to the northern edge of the main tableland and descended a single lane road blasted into the limestone rim. To the left was a solid cliff, to the right was dense fog, but somehow I sensed that there was only this vapor for a long long ways below. We tucked under the fog, and below, my suspicion was confirmed, as there were limestone spires pointing toward us and ready to skewer the entire bus if the driver were to take a sharp right.

The bus ascended and descended other ridges, it passed through the beautifully situated town of San Juan Ixcoy, in its valley setting it could have been in Switzerland. Then on to Soloma, which is in a relatively low area. It is the largest town in the Cuchumatanes, and here I could get a room. It was a Sunday night and the market was winding down. There were people, now drunk, passed out on the sidewalks. The hat of one man, sleeping on his back in the middle of an intersection (this is not too dangerous, as in the northern Cuchumatanes there is an almost total absence of vehicles), had rolled off his head, and laid out of his reach even if he could have moved to get it. I picked it up and placed it on his chest.

I awoke early to catch the 4:00 A.M. bus to San Mateo Ixtatán. The bus was very crowded, so a few other people and I rode on the roof. This has recently been made illegal in Guatemala, but it is still practiced in rural areas. Although it was cold, the crescent Moon and Venus were startlingly beautiful over the slowly brightening horizon. We passed through country of small farms and on to Santa Eulalia, beautifully perched on a hill. Then the road climbed steadily upward into a pine forest and meadows; scenes that reminded me of Colorado mornings. The forest on each side of the road were cut back for a couple of hundred meters, which, according to one source, was to discourage guerrilla ambushes in the 1980s. A bright blue day developed as the bus approached San Mateo Ixtatán.

My interests there were two fold. First, it seemed to be "off the beaten path." It is the most northerly of the highland Cuchumatanes' communities, from here the road goes forever downward to Barrillas. Secondly, according to one author, it is an ancient Chuj Maya site of particular interests. For starters, it is one of only two places in the Highlands, so far from the sea, where salt is obtainable. The salt occurs in brine springs, from which water is taken up and evaporated, the remaining crystals are collected and used in trade. Salt has from time immemorial made this an important site. Today the springs are jealously protected by stout wooden bars, and the salting operation is still alive.

Another feature is the ball court, today's kids use it to play football (soccer), thus, this is possibly the oldest continually in use ball court in the world. Though some rocks have tumbled, the terraces can still be discerned. It is easy to tell that it was once well maintained, and perhaps these terraces doubled as bleachers.

Exploring the steep hillside ruins, which are on a cool ridge overlooking a steamy valley, I saw two women praying and chanting. Beside them was a large wooden cross. I went over to them and realized that they were burning small fires of copal, twigs, and thin yellow candles were broken and lain sideways to simply melt on their fires. Their closed eyes and chanting made them seem to be in a trance. One of the ladies stopped chanting and faced me to talk. I asked her if I could take a picture of her and her friend praying. She shock her head and spoke to me with great command. Then she went back to chanting. The other lady never seemed to be aware that I was there at all. The lady that spoke to me never said a word in Spanish, only Chuj, yet I understood her perfectly. I left them in their peace, but myself a bit unnerved.

But the Catholic church is the most interesting feature. It is one of the oldest churches in the Americas. Usually, friars built churches directly over ancient Indian ruins, and used the stones from the ruins to construct their own churches. This maintained the association of place, and perhaps of material, with the previously established religious authority's command over the local population, thus saving the Spaniards a lot of trouble in reestablishing psychological influence over the local population. This is most clearly observed in Ciudad de México, where the *Zócalo* is built right over the most important Aztec monuments and buildings. However, here in San Mateo Ixtatán, as if out of reverence, admiration, or out of fear of reprisals, the Maya structures were left in tact, and the church built a little up the hill from the main pyramids.

From the outside, though the building is three stories tall, it looks exceedingly squat, and the whole thing seems to want to slide off the hill. The walls are painted a glossy yellow. The arched doorway is trimmed in bright red and in a design that resembles teeth. There are niches with unidentifiable figures with yellow faces and wearing red gowns. The entrance goes through a wall two meters thick. On the back wall are incredibly expressive statues in green and gold trimmed suits. There were four. On the right wall were also four statues. On the left wall were three more statues. It was all I could do not to whip out my camera.

I sat at a pew near the front. I tried to show what reverence I could and kneeled and crossed myself. Settled in I began to spy. There were eight women sitting in pews or on the floor. They had the exact burnings going on as the women outside on the ridge. They looked straight ahead toward the alter and released an incredible amount of emotion. They were so into their own communication with the statues at the front of the church, the Virgin of Guadalupe de Hidalgo and others, that I doubt that they even knew I was there. In fact, I think that I could have exploded firecrackers and they would not have acknowledged me. Some of the women were laughing hysterically, one woman was yelling and weeping and sniffling, others were in deep conversation. Only one man came in and only for a little while. He had a new bandage over a swollen right eye, he said a prayer, deposited some coins in a collection box and went away.

All the talk, crying and laughing seemed to pulsate like a rhythmic chant and I caught myself falling into a timeless state. In Catholic churches, while growing up, I can remember the rhythmic sound and feeling as everyone prayed the same prayer. But in Ixtatán it was different as everyone was on a tangent of their own. It was more individualistic and uninhibited. Even though there were less than a dozen people, their emotional releases made for a powerful atmosphere. In this activity they seemed to actualize themselves, that is, to accomplish something, though intangible, very, very real. These people are very spiritually advanced.

There's not much privacy for a foreigner in Ixtatán. While browsing in the marketplace, someone that I had never seen before came up to me to say that the last bus to Soloma would leave soon and that I better get on it. There are no lodging establishments in Ixtatán.

My time on this trip in Latin America was running out, and although I had good things to look forward to back in Colorado, I was less than excited about the long gruelling journey north. Out of Soloma to Huehuetenango I had to hitchhike as there would not be a bus for a couple of days. I had about 50% success in getting rides, as every other vehicle stopped for me, though these were sometimes an hour apart. I paid a small fee for most of the rides, all of which were for short distances.

From Huehuetenango I took a bus toward the Mexican border on the main branch of the Pan American Highway. We passed through the spectacular gorge of the Río Selegua, the road blasted into a cliff's face. The bus was stopped at one point by a ragtag detachment of the Indian "Civil Patrol," all of us men on the bus had to get out and line up to have our identifications checked. I was the only foreigner, but I was treated as well as the other men. These Civil Patrollers really don't like having to perform this "volunteer" service, as it takes quite a bit of time away from farming and other useful activities, but it is mandatory for them to do so.[32]

At the border at La Mesilla I passed over to México's Ciudad Cuauhtémoc. Immediately I noticed the clean white shirts and uniforms of the Mexican officials, their demeanors were meaner, and all was far more modern than just across the border from where I had come. I boarded a modern bus and we sped off toward the city of San Cristóbal de las Casas, where some months later, on January 1, 1994, two thousand guerrillas lead by the mysterious "Comandante Marcos" would capture the city, along with other major towns, and throw México into chaos.

---

[32]See *Harvest of Violence*, ed. and written in part by Robert Carmack. Norman: University of Oklahoma Press, 1988.

San Cristóbal de las Casas is a major destination for travelers, but I was in too much of a hurry to visit the historic city. The Chiapan highlands are beautiful, but not nearly so mountainous as Guatemala. Night descended. I awoke in the state of Veracruz. Then it was on to *"La Capital"*, and points far, far north.

I entered the United States on a beautiful morning. The border patrolmen, initially not much more enthusiastic in their jobs than the Indian Civil Patrollers in Guatemala, checked my passport and took note of the visas from El Salvador and Nicaragua. They called over a specialist for people coming from there. He asked me a variety of questions about health conditions, the presence of the military, how passing customs goes in those countries, and he was particularly interested in the sea passage in the dugout canoe between El Salvador and Nicaragua. The specialist seemed to look at me as though surprised that I was still alive. I suggested that without his uniform and sidearm he might go and see for himself the area that he is a specialist on.

At the international money exchange in El Paso I was able to convert all the money I had, including a lot of *Cordobas, Quetzals, Lempiras, Colons*, and *Nuevos Pesos*, to a grand total of U.S. $12.00. I walked to the bus station and asked how close to Colorado this sum would get me. The ticket agent laughed and howled, "Not even out of El Paso!" I walked toward the interstate highway comforted by the knowledge that that ticket agent wouldn't get any of my money. What I really needed were two things, one, a free ride, and two, a good sleep. A pickup truck with a mattress in back pulled over. I slept all the way to Albuquerque, kept warm by the New Mexico sun. That night I camped outside of Bernalillo beside the swollen Río Grande. It was filled with melt water from record snows that almost crushed my college into nonexistence that winter, while I was playing around in the sun.

Epilogue

XV.
The Machete

I returned to Central America in October of 1994, not with the intention of adding to this book, or having adventures, but, rather, to publish this book in as short a time as possible, and then to leave. Unfortunately, my efforts were met with frustration. What had seemed like a publishing probability turned into a marathon wait that came to nothing. In the meantime I supported myself by teaching English. I had many good students and made several friends, both international and Guatemalan. In many ways, by working in the country, not for fun or as a volunteer, but just to pay rent and to feed myself, I learnt more about the country than ever before.

However, it all came to an end one tragic day, and although it is completely out of rhythm with the rest of this book, I would be a hypocrite if I were not to recount what happened on that day. The following is from a general letter that I typed up to copy and send to my many scattered friends, so that they would all know what happened to me:

> On December 24th, at 10:00 A.M., I was walking up a trail between Antigua, Guatemala, and the village of El Hato. All was pleasant there in the coffee plantation, and behind me was a beautiful view of Antigua and the three volcanos that surround the city. In Guatemala I had met many very good people, and I was soon to find out just how good, but first I would meet the most dangerous person that I had ever come across.
>
> As I was walking upward, a guy in his mid-twenties caught up to me and walked a step or two behind me, to my left. This was nothing unusual as many people used the five kilometer long trail to go between the city and the village. The only thing that was unusual was that there were very few people around, per-

haps owing to the holiday. I actually spoke to the guy that was walking right behind me, asking him the usual questions that were intended to do little more than to practice my Spanish.

When I realized that there was a rock in the top of my sock, I put my right foot up on an embankment on the edge of the trail to work it out. At that moment I sensed that something was wrong. I looked over my left shoulder and saw a machete arching through the air and coming down on me. I turned to face my attacker and put my left arm above my head to block the blow. With my right hand I pushed him away from me. At that time I hadn't noticed how badly that I was hurt, as I was desperately avoiding his two to four rushes at me while swinging his machete. At some point he managed to strike me on the right palm.

Then, panting, he stood looking at me. It was then that I realized what was happening. I had a shoulder bag which he wanted, and, initially at least, was willing to kill me for. Not knowing what he might do next I took the bag off my shoulder and threw it at him, intending to hit him in the face, but it merely landed at his feet. He picked it up, put it under his arm and ran into the coffee plantation.

As I was out on a day hike, in the bag was an old camera of no value, two bananas, some raisins, chocolate, and a water bottle. He got lunch. Me, I received a cut half way through my left wrist which included breaking the bone, severing tendons, muscles, nerves, and blood vessels. On my right hand I got a deep cut across the palm which affects two fingers.

I pulled off my T-shirt and wrapped it around my left wrist, then pressed my right hand against this bandage. I quickly descended the two kilometers back to Antigua. On the edge of town a van approached me, which I flagged down. It was not hard for the two men in the van to see what I, in a bloody mess, needed. They took me to a clinic in Antigua. Victor, one of the two men, I was to see again.

During the time that I had been in Antigua, I supported myself by teaching English. Two of my students, Antonio and Sabastian, were the sons of Dr. José del Valle Monge, whom I had had several conversations with earlier. In the clinic, angry, confused, and in pain, I asked for him to be called. He came immediately and helped me a great deal. The clinic in Antigua could have patched me up, but I would have had crippled hands for the rest of my life, with only a few usable fingers. I asked José if there were other options. He recommended a hospital in Guatemala City, Herrera Llerandi, where one of his brothers, Dr. Carlos del Valle Monge, was one of the country's top hand surgeons.

At Herrera Llerandi I met Dr. Carlos del Valle Monge, and he instilled in me an unshakable confidence. The microscopic surgery went on for nine and a half hours. When I awoke, I was told that it was believed that the operation had been a complete success. I stayed at the hospital for an additional five days and I was very pleased with the gentleness and kindness shown by the nurses, doctors, and staff. The hospital was spotlessly clean and efficiently run.

I had many visitors. Dale Maki of the U.S. Department of Agriculture (on holiday duty for the State Department) and his family came to see me often, and helped me with calls. Sabastian and Antonio called each day to cheer me up, and visited three times with their father José. One day, José also took Terri and Cristi, my landladies and adoptive parents, to see me. Victor came to see me twice, once with his wife, and once with his two beautiful daughters to remind me that it was worth the effort to recover. My world traveler friend Lieneke, of Holland, came to visit on two occasions. Yasuo, a Japanese student of agricultural economics, and my neighbor, stopped in. My hospital roommate Julio, fluent in both Spanish and English, and in much better condition than me, was a constant help. He always had visitors, whom I enjoyed too.

I got back to New Hampshire, and my own family, on December 31st. Now, January 30, my casts are off and I'm improving quickly. My doctor here feels that I received excellent care in Guatemala. More importantly than my physical condition, though, is how I feel about the crime that befell me. I harbor no ill feelings toward my attacker, and though he has caused me a temporary physical handicap, he shall not cause me a permanent psychological one, and I will continue to travel and to enjoy hiking. Some people, upon hearing of the crime that happened to me, have angrily asserted that if caught, the criminal should be killed. I disagree.

Although the criminal was not caught, and will not be, at least in relation to what he did to me, I feel that he needs help - preferably in prison, so as to keep him from hurting others- but not death, as I feel that the termination of a life is not up to us mortals. In light of Guatemala's several years of savage warfare -for which the United States is partially responsible- and its resultant miserable social state, this criminal needs counselling and education to understand the processes that have led to his sick trade.

One Guatemalan that agrees with me explains that the Indians of Guatemala -for my attacker was an Indian- used to be a pacific people, but the military coup of 1954, that toppled a democratic government, and clearly the work of U.S. companies and the C.I.A. (this is not top secret) set in motion a spiral of violence that has brutalized almost everyone in the country, worsened the poverty of most, left some 200,000 dead, and well over one million fled as refugees (called "illegal aliens" in the U.S.) This is merely a summary of many volumes that could be written. The only wonder is that the little country is no more violent than it is, and the only anger that I feel is toward the imbalances of the world in which we live in.

Although the event just recounted, and time, have altered my attitudes since I wrote the first fourteen chapters of this book, especially as regards security, I have decided not to change anything, as it is an honest travel account, and sometimes painfully so. I have often been asked if I would dare to go back to Latin America, to this I always answer yes. The only thing that I would change in myself there, as I have already done here, is to be more cautious, keep a sharp lookout and don't let anyone get the jump on you.

Since then I have learnt to type again, have done some rock climbing, and am happier than ever to be rowing down the Colorado River again. For all of these activities we need good hands.